THE ROVER BOYS ON THE FARM

OR, LAST DAYS AT PUTNAM HALL

ARTHUR M. WINFIELD

(Edward Stratemeyer)

1st WORLD
LIBRARY
Literary Society

The Rover Boys on the Farm

Arthur M. Winfield

© 1st World Library, 2009
PO Box 2211
Fairfield, IA 52556
www.1stworldlibrary.com
First Edition

LCCN: 2009923383

Softcover ISBN: 978-1-4218-8814-9
Hardcover ISBN: 978-1-4218-8913-9
eBook ISBN: 978-1-4218-8715-9

Purchase *"The Rover Boys on the Farm"*
as a traditional bound book at:
www.1stWorldLibrary.com/purchase.asp?ISBN=978-1-4218-8814-9

1st World Library is a literary, educational organization
dedicated to:

- Creating a free internet library of downloadable ebooks

- Hosting writing competitions and offering book publishing scholarships.

Interested in more 1st World Library books? contact:
literacy@1stworldlibrary.com
Check us out at: www.1stworldlibrary.com

1St World Library Literary Society

Giving Back to the World

"If you want to work on the core problem, it's early school literacy."

- James Barksdale, former CEO of Netscape

"No skill is more crucial to the future of a child, or to a democratic and prosperous society, than literacy."

- Los Angeles Times

"Literacy... means far more than learning how to read and write... The aim is to transmit... knowledge and promote social participation."

- UNESCO

"Literacy is not a luxury, it is a right and a responsibility. If our world is to meet the challenges of the twenty-first century we must harness the energy and creativity of all our citizens."

- President Bill Clinton

"Parents should be encouraged to read to their children, and teachers should be equipped with all available techniques for teaching literacy, so the varying needs and capacities of individual kids can be taken into account."

- Hugh Mackay

PREFACE

MY DEAR BOYS: With this I present to you "The Rover Boys on the Farm," the twelfth volume in the "Rover Boys Series for Young Americans."

It is a large number of volumes to write about one set of characters, isn't it? When I started the series, many years ago, I had in mind, as I have told you before, to pen three books, possibly four. But as soon as I had written "The Rover Boys at School," "The Rover Boys on the Ocean," and "The Rover Boys in the Jungle," there was a cry for more, and so I wrote "The Rover Boys Out West," "On the Great Lakes," "In the Mountains," "On Land and Sea," "In Camp," "On the River," "On the Plains," and then "In Southern Waters," where we last left our heroes.

In the present story, as promised in the last volume, the scene is shifted back to the farm and to dear old Putnam Hall, with their many pleasant associations. As before, Sam, Tom and Dick are to the front, along with several of their friends, and there are a number of adventures, some comical and some strange and mystifying. At the school the rivalries are as keen as ever, but the Rover boys are on their mettle, and prove their worth on more than one occasion.

Again I thank my numerous readers for all the kind words

they have spoken about my stories. I hope the present volume will please them in every way.

Affectionately and sincerely yours,

EDWARD STRATEMEYER

CONTENTS

CHAPTER I

SOMETHING ABOUT THE ROVER BOYS

"Sam, this isn't the path."

"I know it, Tom."

"We've missed our way," went on Tom Rover, with a serious look on his usually sunny face.

"It looks that way to me," answered Sam Rover, his younger brother. "I think we made a wrong turn after we slid down the cliff."

"What is keeping Dick?"

"I don't know."

"Let's call to him," went on Tom, and set up a loud cry, in which his brother joined. The pair listened intently, but no answer came back.

"I don't like this," said Sam, an anxious look in his clear eyes. "Maybe Dick is in trouble."

"Perhaps so," answered Tom Rover.

The two boys were far up on a mountainside, and all around them were tall trees, thick brushwood, and immense ridges of rocks. It had been a clear, sunshiny day, but now the sky was overcast, and it looked like rain.

"We've got to go back for Dick," said Tom, after a painful pause. "No use of going on without him."

"I hope he hasn't fallen over some cliff and hurt himself," returned his younger brother.

"I don't see why he doesn't answer us, if he's all right," was the unsatisfactory reply. "Come on, or the storm will over-take us before we get down from the mountain and we'll be soaked by the time we reach home."

Side by side the brothers retraced their steps—a hard task, for it is much easier to climb down a steep mountainside than to climb up.

To those who have read the previous volumes in this "Rover Boys Series," the two brothers just mentioned will need no special introduction. The Rover boys were three in number, Dick being the oldest, fun-loving Tom coming next, and Sam bringing up the rear. All were bright, lively, up-to-date lads, and honest and manly to the core. They lived on a farm called Valley Brook, in New York state,—a beautiful spot owned by their uncle, Randolph Rover, and his wife, Martha. Their father, Anderson Rover, also lived at the farm when at home, but he was away a great deal on business.

From the farm the boys had been sent, some years before, to Putnam Hall, an ideal place of learning, of which we shall learn more as our tale proceeds. What the lads did there on their arrival has already been related in "The Rover Boys at School," the first volume of this series.

Arthur M. Winfield

A short term at Putnam Hall was followed by a trip on the ocean, and then a long journey to the jungles of Africa, in search of Anderson Rover, who had disappeared. Then came a grand outing out west, and another outing on the great lakes, followed by some stirring adventures in the mountains of New York state.

Coming from the mountains, the three youths had expected to go back to Putnam Hall at once, but fate ordained otherwise and they were cast away in the Pacific Ocean, as related in "The Rover Boys on Land and Sea." They had a hard task of it getting home, and then returned to the school and had some splendid times while in camp with the other cadets.

When vacation was once more at hand the boys soon solved the problem of what to do. Their Uncle Randolph had taken a houseboat for debt. The craft was located on the Ohio River, and it was resolved to make a trip down the Mississippi.

"It will be the best ever!" Tom declared, and they started with much enthusiasm, taking with them "Songbird" Powell, a school chum addicted to the making of doggerel which he called poetry, Fred Garrison, a plucky boy who had stood by them through thick and thin, and Hans Mueller, a German youth who was still struggling with the mysteries of the English tongue. With the boys went an old friend, Mrs. Stanhope, and her sister, Mrs. Laning. With Mrs. Stanhope was her only daughter Dora, whom Dick Rover considered the sweetest girl in the whole world, and Mrs. Laning had with her two daughters, Grace and Nellie, especial friends of Sam and Dick.

The trip on the houseboat proved a long and eventful one, and during that time the boys and their company fell in with

Dan Baxter, Lew Flapp and several other enemies. On the Mississippi the craft was damaged, and while it was being repaired the party took a trip inland, as related in "The Rover Boys on the Plains." Then the houseboat was stolen, and what this led to has been related in detail in "The Rover Boys in Southern Waters." In that volume they brought to book several of the rascals who had annoyed them, and they caused Dan Baxter to feel so ashamed of himself that the bully made up his mind to reform.

Tired out from their long trip, the Rover boys were glad enough to get back home again. For nearly a week their friends remained with them at Valley Brook farm and then they departed, the Stanhopes and Lanings for their homes and Fred, Hans and Songbird for Putnam Hall.

"Of course you're coming back to the Hall?" Fred had said on leaving.

"Coming back?" had been Tom's answer. "Why, you couldn't keep us away with a Gatling gun!"

"To be sure we'll be back," answered Dick Rover.

"And we'll have the greatest times ever," chimed in Sam. "I am fairly aching to see the dear old school again."

"And Captain Putnam, and all the rest," continued Tom.

"And have some fun, eh, Tom?" and Sam poked his fun-loving brother in the ribs.

"Well, when we go back we've got to do some studying," Dick had put in. "Do you know what father said yesterday?"

"No, what?" came simultaneously from his brothers.

"He said we were getting too old to go to Putnam Hall—that we ought to be thinking of going to college, or of getting into business."

"Hum!" murmured Tom, and he became suddenly thoughtful.

"I know why he said that," said Sam, with a wink at his big brother. "He knows how sweet Dick is on Dora, and—"

"Hi! you let up!" cried Dick, his face reddening. "It wasn't that at all. We are getting pretty old for Putnam Hall, and you know it."

"It seems I'd never want to leave the dear old school," murmured Tom. "Why, it's like a second home to us. Think of all the jolly times we've had there—and the host of friends we've made."

"And the enemies," added Sam. "Don't forget them, or they may feel slighted."

"Dan Baxter was our worst enemy in that school, and he is going to reform, Sam."

"Perhaps. I won't feel sure of it until I really see it," answered the youngest Rover.

"By the way, I got a postal from Dan to-day," said Dick. "He is in Philadelphia, and working for a carpet manufacturer."

"Well, if he's gone to work, that's a good sign," said Tom.

On their arrival at the farm the boys had been met by their father, but now Anderson Rover had gone away on a business trip which was to last for several days. As usual, he left the lads in charge of his brother and the boys' aunt.

"Now just take it easy for awhile," was Mr. Rover's advice, on leaving. "Rest up all you can, and then, when you go back to the school, you'll feel as bright as a dollar."

"Silver or paper, dad?" asked Tom, mischievously.

"Now, Tom—"

"Oh, I know what you mean, dad, and I'll be as quiet as a mule with a sandbag tied to his tail," answered the fun-loving offspring.

The day after Anderson Rover's departure from the farm was quiet enough, but on the morning following the boys' uncle received a letter in the mail which seemed to trouble him not a little.

"I must attend to this matter without delay," said Randolph Rover to his wife.

"What is wrong, Randolph?"

"I don't think I can explain to you, Martha. It's about those traction company bonds I purchased a few months ago."

"Those you paid ten thousand dollars for?"

"Yes."

"What about them?"

"As I said before, I can't explain—it is rather a complicated affair."

"They are yours, aren't they, Randolph?"

"Oh, yes. But—"

"Aren't they worth what you gave for them?"

"I hope so."

"Can't you find out and make sure?"

"That is what I am going to do," replied Randolph Rover, and heaved a deep sigh. As my old readers know, he was a very retired individual, given to scientific research, especially in regard to farming, and knew little about business.

"If you've been swindled in any way, you must go after the men who sold you the bonds," said Mrs. Rover. "We cannot afford to lose so much money."

"I don't believe I've been swindled—at least, if I have, I think the party who sold me the bonds will make them good, Martha. I'll know all about it to-morrow," answered Randolph Rover, and there the conversation came to an end.

CHAPTER II

WHAT HAPPENED ON THE MOUNTAIN

It was on the day that Randolph Rover was to go to the town of Carwell, fifteen miles away, to see about the bonds, that the three Rover boys planned for a day's outing.

"Let us go to the top of Chase Mountain," suggested Sam. "I haven't been up there for three years."

"Second the suggestion," replied Tom. "We can take a lunch along and make a day of it," and so it was arranged.

Chase Mountain was about three miles away, on the other side of Humpback Falls, where Sam had once had such a stirring adventure, as told in detail in "The Rover Boys at School." It was a ragged eminence, and from the top a view could be had of the country for many miles around.

The day seemed to be a perfect one when the three youths started, and when they reached the top of the mountain they enjoyed the vast panorama spread before them. They likewise enjoyed the substantial lunch their Aunt Martha had provided, and ate until Tom was ready to "bust his buttons," as he expressed it.

Arthur M. Winfield

"Let us try a new path down," said Sam, when it came time to go home, and he and Tom led the way, over a series of rocky ridges and cliffs anything but easy to traverse. In some places they had to drop ten and fifteen feet, and once Tom came down on his ankle in a manner that made him cry with pain.

"You look out for yourself," warned Dick. "If you sprain an ankle up here we'll have a job of it getting you home."

"No sprained ankle for mine, thank you," replied Tom. And he was more careful after that.

As Dick came after his brothers he saw something peculiar at one side of the path he was pursuing. It appeared to be a tin lunch box suspended from a tree limb by a bit of wire. The box was painted red and seemed to be new.

"That's strange," said the eldest Rover boy to himself. "Who would leave such a thing as that in that position? I'll have to investigate."

Without telling Sam and Tom what he was going to do, Dick left the path and plunged into the bushes which grew between himself and the tree from which the tin box was suspended. Among the bushes the footing was uncertain, and hardly had he taken a dozen steps when he felt himself sinking.

"Hi! this won't do!" he cried in alarm, and then plunged down into a big hole, some bushes, moss and dead leaves coming down on top of him.

In the meantime, Sam and Tom had gone on. Coming to where the path appeared to divide, they turned to the right, only to find, five minutes later, that they had made a mistake.

"Where in the world can Dick be?" murmured Sam, after he and his brother had called again. "I thought he was right behind us."

"So did I, Sam. It's mighty queer what's become of him. If he fell over a cliff—" Tom did not finish, but heaved a deep sigh.

With anxious hearts the two boys endeavored to retrace their steps up the mountainside. They had to climb up one of the cliffs, and just as this was accomplished it began to rain.

"More bad luck," grumbled Sam. "If this keeps on we'll soon be soaked."

"Spit, spat, spo! Where did that mountain path go!" cried Tom, repeating a doggerel often used by children. "Dick! Dick!" he yelled, at the top of his lungs. Then Sam joined in the call once again. But as before, there was no answer.

It must be confessed that the two Rover boys were now thoroughly alarmed. As they had climbed up the mountainside they knew they must be close to the spot where they had last seen Dick. What had become of their big brother?

"Tom, do you think he could have fallen over some cliff and rolled to the bottom of the mountain?" questioned Sam, anxiously.

"How could he roll to the bottom with the trees so thick? He would have plenty of chance to catch hold of one of them."

"Not if he was knocked unconscious."

"Well, where can he be?"

Arthur M. Winfield

"I don't know."

It was now raining steadily, and to protect themselves the two boys pulled their caps well down over their heads and turned up their coat collars. They came to a halt under the wide-spreading branches of a hemlock tree.

"It beats the nation, that's what it does," declared Tom. "Maybe the earth opened and swallowed him up!"

"Tom, this is no joke."

"And I'm not joking, Sam. I can't understand it at all."

"Is that the path over yonder?" continued the youngest Rover, pointing to a spot beyond the opposite side of the hemlock tree.

"It looks a little like it," was Tom's reply. "Might as well go over and make sure."

Leaving the shelter of the tree, they made their way through the bushes, which were now beginning to drip from the rain. As they progressed Sam pushed a big branch from him and let it swing back suddenly, thereby catching Tom full in the face.

"Wow!" spluttered the fun-loving Rover, as he staggered back. "Hi! Sam, do you think I need a shower bath? I'm wet enough already." And Tom commenced to brush the water from his face.

"I didn't mean to let it slip," answered Sam. "But say—"

What Sam was going to say further will never be known, for just then he felt himself slipping down into some sort of a hole. He tried to leap back, and made a clutch at Tom's legs, and the next instant both rolled over and over and shot downward, out of the daylight into utter darkness.

They were taken so completely by surprise that neither said a word. Over and over they went, a shower of dirt, sticks and dead leaves coming after them. Then they brought up on a big pile of decayed leaves and lay there, the breath all but knocked out of them.

"Wha—what—where are we?" gasped Sam, when he felt able to speak.

"Say, is thi—this a ne—new shoot-the—the—chutes?" asked Tom who was bound to have his fun no matter what occurred.

"Are you hurt?"

"I don't think I am, but I reckon my liver turned over about ten times. How about you?"

"Shook up, that's all," answered Sam, after rising to his feet. "Say, we came down in a hurry, didn't we?"

"Yes, and got no return ticket either." Tom looked upward. "Gracious! the top of this hole is about fifty feet away! We are lucky that we didn't break our necks!"

"Now we are down here, the question is, How do we get out, Tom?"

"Don't ask me any conundrums."

"We've got to get out somehow."

"Unless we want to stay here and save the expense of a cemetery lot."

"Tom!"

"Oh, I know it's no joke, Sam. But what is there to do? Here's a hole at least fifty feet deep and the sides are almost perpendicular. Do you think we can climb up? I am afraid, if we try it, we'll end by breaking our necks."

"It certainly is steep," answered the youngest brother, looking upward. "Say!" he added, suddenly, "do you suppose Dick went down in some such hole as this?"

"Perhaps; where there is one hole there may be more. If he went down let us hope he didn't get killed."

As well as they were able, the two boys gazed around them. The hole was irregular in form, but about fifteen feet in diameter. One side was of rough rocks and the other dirt and tree roots. At the top the treacherous bushes overhung all sides of the opening, partly concealing the yawning pit below.

"The rain is coming in pretty lively," was Sam's comment, presently. "I wonder if there is any danger of this hole filling up with water."

"I don't think so, but if it does we can swim out."

"Or get drowned."

"Now who is getting blue?" demanded Tom.

To keep out of the worst of the rain Sam leaned against one of the sides of the hole. He felt it give beneath his weight and before he could save himself he went down into another hole, and Tom came after him.

The boys were scared and both cried out lustily. They did not fall far, however—in fact, they rather rolled, for the second opening was on a slant of forty-five degrees. They brought up against something soft, but this time it was not a bank of decayed leaves.

"Sam! And Tom!"

"Dick!"

"Where did you come from?"

"How did you get here?"

"Are you hurt?"

"No, are you?"

"No."

These were some of the questions asked and answered as the three Rover boys stared at each other. Other questions quickly followed, and Dick told how he had started to get the tin box and gone down so unexpectedly.

"You want to be careful," he cautioned. "This mountainside is full of holes and pitfalls. I came down one hole and then shot right into another."

"And we did the same thing!" cried Tom. "Thank heaven none of us have broken bones!"

"Didn't you hear us call to you?" asked the youngest Rover.

"I thought I heard something—but I was not sure. I called back."

"We didn't hear you," answered Tom.

Dick had been trying to get out of the hole into which he had tumbled, but without success. Now the sides were growing slippery from the rain, so the ascent became more difficult than ever.

"We're in a pickle," sighed Sam.

"Oh, we've got to get out somehow," answered his big brother. "We can't stay here forever."

The opening was almost square, with three sides of rough rock. In trying to climb up some of the rocks Tom gave one a shove and it slid from sight, revealing an opening beyond.

"Hullo! another hole!" cried the youth, leaping back in consternation. "Why, the old mountain is fairly honeycombed with them."

"I was never on this side of the mountain before," said Dick. "They used to tell some queer stories about this side."

"Didn't they say some parts were haunted?" asked Sam.

"Yes, and it was said that, years ago, many travelers coming this way disappeared."

"Well, why shouldn't they, with so many holes around?" came from Tom. "If we get out alive we'll be lucky."

With great care they got down on their hands and knees and examined the opening beyond the rocks.

"I believe it's a big cave," announced Dick a few minutes later. "And if it is, I'm rather inclined to look around inside. Perhaps it will lead to some opening on the mountainside where we can get out."

Arthur M. Winfield

CHAPTER III

A MYSTERIOUS CAVE

At first Sam and Tom demurred to entering the cave—which looked dark and forbidding. But Dick insisted that he was going ahead, and rather than be left behind they went along.

"We'll light some kind of a torch," said the eldest Rover. "Got some matches?"

"Yes, I brought along a pocketful," answered Sam. "Didn't know but what we'd want to build a campfire this noon."

"We'll want one now—to dry our clothing by," said Tom. "Let us pick up the driest of the sticks."

This they did, and having entered the cave, they made a good-sized blaze. This sent a ruddy glow around the cavern, and as the boys moved about fantastic shadows went dancing on the rocky walls, adding to the weirdness of the scene.

From the fire each of the youths provided himself with a torch, and thus equipped they moved around the cave with care, taking precautions not to fall into any more holes. They soon found the opening on the mountainside long and narrow and running downward.

"We don't want to get lost," cautioned Sam.

"Oh, we can always go back to the fire," answered Dick.

"Unless it goes out on us."

"It won't burn itself out for an hour—I saw to that before we left it."

As the boys advanced into the cave they came across a heap of bones. Dick examined them carefully.

"Skeletons?" queried Sam, and his voice trembled slightly.

"Yes—of lambs and pigs," was the dry answer. "Somebody has been making this a rendezvous and living on the fat of the land."

"Maybe that accounts for Jerry Burden's losses," suggested Tom. "He said he lost a lamb last spring, and two pigs."

"Yes, and old Richard Feltham lost a pig and some chickens," added Dick. "Maybe this has been a hangout for tramps."

"Do you think they are here still?" questioned Sam. "We don't want to have any trouble."

"I am sure I don't know, Sam. But this proves one thing."

"That we can get out of the cave?"

"Exactly. See, here is an old coat and a pair of old shoes. Somebody has been in the habit of coming here—and he wasn't in the habit of getting in the way we got in."

They moved on, and soon reached a larger opening. Here they found a bit of old harness and, further on, where the ground was soft, the tracks of wagon wheels.

"Somebody has been in the habit of driving right in here!" exclaimed Tom. "We are sure to get out!" and his face showed his relief.

"Hark! what's that?" cried Sam, and shrank back as a strange rumbling was heard. "Is it an earthquake, or a landslide?"

"It's thunder, that's all," said Dick, a minute later, as they listened.

"To be sure—the storm was on us when we fell into the first hole," answered the youngest Rover.

"Perhaps we can be glad we are under shelter—if the storm is going to be a bad one," came from Tom. "But, come on, I want to see daylight again."

He moved on and then gave a cry of astonishment.

"Look!"

His brothers did so. On one side of the cave were piled thirty or forty packing cases. The majority of them were empty, but three, directed to one Jackson Dwight, Carwell, were full and nailed up.

"Well, I never!" murmured Sam. "Dick—"

"The freight thieves!" ejaculated the eldest Rover. "Don't you remember what was in the paper before we went south, and what was in again only yesterday? They have been missing freight from Carwell and Boxton and half a dozen other stations for over a year. The thieves must have brought their stuff here and then taken some of it from the packing cases and carted it away again."

"It certainly looks like it," answered Tom. "Only three full cases left. I wonder when these were taken?"

"Most likely only a short time ago," said Dick. "The cases look new."

"Do you suppose any of the freight thieves are around? If they are we want to keep out of their way—if they are desperate characters."

They moved on, and then Dick called a sudden halt.

"I can see daylight ahead," he said. "And somebody is moving around. Let us put out the torches."

His suggestion was speedily followed, and the three Rover boys advanced with caution. At its outer end the cave became broader while the roof was only about ten feet high.

"Hullo, here's another surprise," whispered Dick, as they came closer to the opening. "Look at that!"

He pointed to one side of the cave and there the others saw an automobile runabout standing and on the seat two men dressed for a tour. They were talking to a third man, who was lounging against a front wheel, smoking a brier-root pipe.

"Maybe they are the freight thieves," whispered Tom. "Let us get out of sight and listen to what they have to say."

It was an easy matter to keep out of sight, for the walls of the cave were very uneven at this point. They got behind a projection, and by crawling up a rocky ledge managed to reach a point above and to one side of the runabout and not over a dozen feet from it.

"Then you weren't going to stop here, Merrick?" asked the man leaning against the wheel.

"Not now, Dangler," was the reply of the man with the pipe. "The storm drove us in here."

"When do you expect to meet this Randolph Rover?"

"Very soon."

"He ought to be easy—he is so simple minded."

"Oh, I think we can work him right enough," put in the third man, who was tall and thin-cheeked.

"Well, if you do, don't forget that I get my share, Pike," said the man called Dangler.

"Haven't you always gotten your share?" demanded Pike.

"I suppose I have."

"And haven't we given you the information whenever any valuable freight was coming this way?" put in the man called Merrick.

"Yes, and got your full share of the proceeds, while I ran the risk," growled Dangler. "It's getting dangerous—I'm going to quit—after the next big haul," went on the man with the pipe.

"All right—as you wish," answered Merrick. "I wish this

storm would let up. The road will be something fierce for our runabout."

"And bad for my wagon," growled Dangler in return.

The boys listened to the conversation with deep interest. The reference to their uncle amazed them, and they wondered what the two men in the runabout had in mind to do. By their talk it was evident they meant to accomplish something unlawful.

"They are going to play Uncle Randolph some trick," whispered Sam. "We must get home and warn him."

"What we ought to do is to have the whole crowd arrested," answered Tom. "They are all implicated in the theft of freight."

"That's the talk," said Dick. "The question is, How can we do it? We are no match for those three men, and more than likely they are armed."

After this the three men conversed in such a low tone the boys could not hear a quarter of what was said. But they learned enough to know that Merrick and Pike were going to meet their uncle and play him false in some way, and they heard the words "traction bonds" and "coupons" several times.

"Uncle Randolph had ten thousand dollars' worth of traction company bonds," said Dick. "He bought them only a short while ago. They pay five and a half per cent. interest and he thought them a first-class investment."

"Oh, we'll have to warn him," said Sam. "He is so open-hearted he would trust most anybody."

Merrick had descended from the runabout and gone out of the cave. Now he came back, said something to the others, and started up the auto. In another moment he had the machine turned around. Then it spun out of the cave and down a fairly good road in the direction of Carwell. The man named Dangler followed the runabout to the road and watched it disappear around a turn bordered by trees. The storm was now rolling away to the westward and the rain had ceased.

"They have gone!" cried Tom. "Where to?"

"Perhaps to our farm—to see Uncle Randolph," answered Sam. "We ought to follow them as quickly as we can."

"I think we had better capture the fellow left behind," said Dick. "We ought to be able to do it."

"That's the talk," said Tom. "Sure we can do it, being three to one."

Dangler watched the runabout and then gazed up and down the mountain for several minutes. Then of a sudden he started in a direction opposite to that taken by the machine.

"He is going away!" cried Sam.

"Come on after him!" called his big brother, and ran from the cave with the others at his heels. Just as he did this Dangler glanced back and saw them.

"Hey, you!" he cried in consternation.

"Stop!" called out Dick. "We want you."

At this command Dangler was more amazed than ever. But

of a sudden he appeared to realize something of what had happened and commenced to run.

"Stop!" cried Tom and Sam, but at this the man only ran the faster.

"Come on—we've got to catch that rascal!" exclaimed Dick, and started to sprint. The others followed as quickly as they could, and a rapid chase along the mountain road ensued. But if the boys could run so could the freight robber, and he made the best possible use of his legs until he gained a side trail. Then he darted into this, and when the Rover boys came up he had disappeared.

"Where is he?" panted Sam.

"He took to this path, but he isn't in sight," answered Dick. He was almost winded himself.

"Come on, he must be somewhere around," put in Tom, and ran down the path several hundred feet. Then he tripped over a fallen log and went headlong in the bushes and wet grass. He got up looking tired out and cross.

"We've missed him," announced Dick, rather dismally. "It's a pity, too. He deserves to be put under arrest."

"I think we had better get home and warn Uncle Randolph," returned Sam. "If we don't there is no telling what that fellow Merrick and that Pike may do."

CHAPTER IV

AT THE FARM

The others considered Sam's advice good, and after another look around for Dangler, they turned in the direction of home. They were a good three miles from the farm and had to cross the river above the falls, thus adding half a mile more to the journey. It was wet and muddy walking and they had not covered over a mile when Tom called a halt.

"I am about fagged out," he announced. "Wonder if we can't hire a buggy at the next farmhouse."

"We can try anyway," answered Dick.

Directly after crossing the river they came to a small farmhouse, and walked around to the kitchen, where they saw an old woman shelling peas.

"We can't let you have any carriage," she said. "The men folks are to town and they've got the horses."

The boys were about to turn away when Dick thought of something.

"By the way, do you know a man named Dangler?" he asked.

"Sure, I do," was the answer.

"Does he live around here?"

"I guess he lives where he pleases. He is an old bachelor and comes and goes as he likes. He used to have a cottage down the pike, but it burnt down last winter."

"Then you haven't any idea where he is stopping now?"

"No."

"Do you know a man named Merrick and another man named Pike?" went on the eldest Rover boy.

At this the old woman shook her head.

"Never heard tell of them," she said.

"Has this Dangler any relatives around here?" asked Tom.

"None that I know of."

"Do you know what kind of man he is?" asked Sam.

"I never talk about my neighbors," answered the old woman, and drew up her thin lips and went on shelling peas.

Feeling it would be useless to ask any more questions, the three boys journeyed wearily on to the next farmhouse. This belonged to a fat German named Gus Schmidt, who knew the Rovers fairly well.

"Yah, I let you haf a carriage alretty," said Gus Schmidt. "Put you must pring him back to-morrow, hey?"

Arthur M. Winfield

"We will," answered Dick.

"I vos hear some putty goot stories apout you Rofer poys," went on Mr. Schmidt, while he was hooking up his horse. "You vos on der Mississippi Rifer, hey?"

"We were," answered Sam.

"Und you vos go owid on der blains und catch some counter-feiters, hey?"

"Yes, we had something to do with it," came from Tom.

"Und den you vos go py der Gulluf of Mexico alretty und find a steampoat vos has nopotty got on it," pursued Gus Schmidt. "Ach, it vos vonderful vot vos habben to somepody, ain't it?"

"Didn't you ever have anything happen to you, Mr. Schmidt?" asked Sam.

"Only vonce, und dot vos enough. I peen in New York, und der poys call me names. Den I run after dem, und da vos go py a cellar full of vater. I vos run on a poard, und der poys turn dot poard—"

"And you fell into the water," finished Tom.

"Not much! I chumped back to der sidevalk," answered Gus Schmidt, and then laughed heartily at his little joke.

The three Rover boys were soon in the carriage and on the way to the farm. The horse that had been loaned to them was a speedy animal and they made good time despite the muddi-ness of the road. The brief storm had been a severe one, and in one spot the roadbed was considerably washed out.

The boys took the carriage around to the barn and left it in charge of Jack Ness, the man of all work. Then they hurried to the house.

"Oh, boys, I am so glad that you are back!" exclaimed Mrs. Rover, on seeing them. "I suppose you are wet through. Better dry your clothing at once, or change them, and I'll get you some hot tea to drink."

"We are all right, Aunt Martha," answered Dick. "We were under shelter during the worst of the storm. Is Uncle Randolph around?"

"No, he went to Carwell on business. I am worried about him, for I am afraid he got caught in the storm, for he drove over."

"What did he go for?" questioned Tom, quickly.

"Oh, it was a private matter."

"About some traction company bonds?" asked Sam, who could not hold back his curiosity.

"Yes. But how do you happen to know about it?" demanded his aunt, in astonishment.

"We found something out to-day, aunty," said Dick. "It's a queer piece of business. Do you know where Uncle Randolph was going?"

"You mean in Carwell?"

"Yes."

"I think to the hotel."

"Hum," mused the eldest of the Rover boys. "Wonder if I can get him on the telephone?" For a telephone line had been put up from Oak Run to the farm.

"Why, Dick, is there anything wrong?" demanded Mrs. Rover, turning pale.

"I hope not, Aunt Martha. We'll soon know. Don't worry, please."

"Your uncle was very much disturbed when he went away."

"I am going to try to telephone to him at once," said Dick.

The telephone was on a landing of the stairs, where the bell could readily be heard upstairs and down, and Dick lost no time in taking down the receiver and calling up the office at Oak Run.

"I want to get the hotel at Carwell," he told the operator. "This is 685 W," he added.

"I cannot give you Carwell," was the answer.

"Why not?"

"The lightning struck down some of our poles and the line is out of commission."

This was dismaying news and for the moment Dick was nonplussed. Then he spoke to the operator again.

"Can you reach Farleytown?"

"Yes, but the line from Farleytown to Carwell is down, too," came over the wire.

"Can you reach Deeming's Corners?"

"No. Can't get to Carwell in any way at all," was the decided answer, and Dick hung up the receiver much crestfallen.

"The storm has knocked the telephone service into a cocked hat," he explained to the others. "The only way for us to reach Carwell is to drive there."

"Then let us do that, and right away!" cried Tom, who had been talking to his aunt. "Uncle Randolph took those ten thousand dollars worth of traction company bonds with him, and Aunt Martha says the bonds were unregistered, so anybody could use them."

"Do you think somebody is going to steal the bonds?" asked the aunt.

"Two men are up to some game,—that is as much as we know," said Dick, thinking it unwise to keep his aunt in the dark any longer. "And we know the men are rascals," he added.

"Oh, will they—they attack your uncle?"

"I don't think they are that kind," said Sam. "I think they'll try to get the bonds away by some slick game."

The aunt hated to see the boys go on a mission of possible peril and yet she wanted to have her husband warned. The lads ran down to the barn and had Jack Ness hitch up a fresh team to a buckboard. It was now growing dark.

"Take good care of yourselves," cried Mrs. Rover, as they drove off. "If the telephone and telegraph poles are down on the road see that you do not run into any of them."

They were driving to the gateway of the big farm when they saw Alexander Pop running after them, flourishing something in his hand. Aleck was a colored man who had once worked at Putnam Hall, but who was now attached to the Rover household.

"I was jess a-thinkin' that maybe yo' boys wasn't armed," he said. "If yo' ain't, don't yo' want dis pistol?" And he held up a weapon he had purchased while on the river trip with them.

"I didn't think there would be any shooting," answered Dick. "But now you've brought it, I might as well take the pistol along," and he placed the weapon in his pocket.

"Perhaps yo' would like to hab dis chicken along?" went on the colored man. He delighted to be with the Rover boys on every possible occasion.

"No, the buckboard is crowded now," answered Dick. "You do what you can to quiet Mrs. Rover."

"Yes, tell her not to worry about us," added Tom.

"And don't mention the pistol," called Sam, as the turnout moved on again.

After leaving the vicinity of the farm, the boys had a distance of thirteen miles to cover. Part of the road lay through the valley which had given the farm its name, but then it ran up and over a series of hills, and through several patches of woods. Under the trees it was dark, and they had to slacken their speed for fear of accident.

"Danger ahead!" cried Sam presently, and Dick, who was driving, brought the team to a halt. Across the road lay an uprooted tree.

"Can't drive around that," announced Sam, after an inspection. "And it will be hard work dragging it out of the way."

"We'll drive over it," announced Dick. "Hold tight, if you don't want to be bounced off."

He called to the horses, and the team moved forward slowly. They had not been out of the stable for several days and were inclined to dance and prance. They stepped in among the tree branches and then one animal reared and tried to back.

"Get up there, Dan!" cried Dick. "None of that tomfoolery! Get up, I say!"

The other horse wanted to go ahead, and he dragged his mate deeper into the tree limbs. Then, without warning, the balky animal made a leap, cleared the tree, and started down the road at breakneck speed.

"Look out, the team is running away!" yelled Sam, and then stopped short, for he as well as the others were in danger of being thrown from the buckboard.

Arthur M. Winfield

CHAPTER V

RANDOLPH ROVER'S STORY

It was a time of peril, and all of the Rover boys realized this fully. The buckboard was a strong one, but the road had been washed out so much by the storm that it was very uneven, and the jouncing threatened each moment to land one lad or another out on his head.

"Whoa! whoa!" yelled Dick, and did his best to rein in the team. But, as mentioned before, they had not been out for several days and were consequently fresh and inclined to keep on. Each had the bit in his teeth, so pulling on the lines was of little avail.

"If we don't stop soon something is going to happen," was Tom's comment, and scarcely had he spoken when they went down into a rut and Sam was flung up and over a wheel into some brushwood. Then the team went on as before.

The woods left behind, they came to a large open field, where the ground was rather soft.

"Turn in here, Dick, if you can," cried Tom.

"That is what I am trying to do," answered the eldest Rover

boy, pulling on one rein with might and main.

At first the horses refused to leave the road, but at last the strain on the one rein told and Dan swerved to the right, dragging his mate with him. As the wheels of the buckboard sank into the soft soil of the field the pulling became harder, and at last the horses dropped into a walk and were then brought to a stop with ease.

"Wonder if Sam was hurt?" were Dick's first words, as he leaped to the ground and ran to the heads of the team to quiet them.

"He went out in a hurry, that's sure," was Tom's answer. "Can you hold them now?"

"Yes—the fire is all out of them."

"Then I'll run back and see to Sam." And Tom set off on a dog trot toward the spot where the mishap to his younger brother had occurred. He found Sam sitting on a rock rubbing his left wrist.

"Hurt?" he sang out, anxiously.

"This wrist is a little lame, and my knee is skinned," was the answer. "Did they get away and throw you out?"

"No, Dick managed to stop them by turning into a soft field. It is lucky you didn't break your neck."

"I might have if I hadn't tumbled into the bushes, Tom. Gracious, how the buckboard did jounce up and down!"

Limping a little on account of the bruised knee, Sam followed his brother down the road. They found Dick had led the team from the field. He, too, was glad to learn Sam was not seriously injured.

"What's to do now?" asked Tom. "I don't like to trust that team much."

"Oh, they're tamed down now," asserted Dick. "I am sure they won't want to run away again."

"We want to get to Carwell as soon as possible, but we don't want to do it by breaking our necks," went on the fun-loving Rover.

Once more the three youths got on the buckboard and Dick started the team. The fire was now all out of them, and they went along at their regular gait. It had grown so dark the boys had to light a lantern they had brought along.

"Listen!" said Sam presently, and held up his hand. From out of the darkness they heard the steady chug-chug of an automobile. It seemed to be coming toward them.

"Maybe it's the runabout with those two men!" cried Tom.

"If it is, let us try to stop them," answered Dick.

They brought the team to a halt and listened. For a few seconds the chug-chug came closer, then it died away in the distance on their left.

"The machine must have taken to a side road," was Dick's comment.

"Yes, and we may as well go on," answered Tom.

Once more they proceeded on their way. Less than a hundred

yards were covered when they reached the side road. In the muddy roadway the tracks of the rubber tires of the automobile were plainly to be seen.

"If we were sure they were the men we might go after them," said Sam.

"We'd not catch them with the horses," answered Dick.

"And it might be another machine," added Tom. "There are plenty of them in Carwell."

They were now within two miles of the town and the farm-houses were becoming more numerous. Just as they struck a paved street, Tom uttered an exclamation:

"Here comes Uncle Randolph now!"

He pointed ahead to where a street light fell on a horse and buggy. On the seat of the latter sat Randolph Rover, driving along contentedly.

"Hullo, Uncle Randolph!" sang out Dick, and brought the buckboard to a halt.

"Why, Dick!" exclaimed the uncle, staring at the three boys in surprise. "What brings you here this time of night?"

"We came to find you, Uncle Randolph," said Tom, and added: "Are your traction company bonds safe?"

"My bonds? What do you know of my bonds?" And now the buggy halted beside the buckboard.

"We know two men are after them," said Sam.

"Oh, I thought that was a secret," answered Mr. Rover.

"But did you see the men?" asked Dick, impatiently.

"Oh, yes, and I have had a narrow escape from being swindled," answered the uncle, calmly.

"Oh, then you escaped," said Dick, and he and his brothers breathed a sigh of relief.

"Yes, I escaped," answered Randolph Rover. "It was very kind of Mr. Jardell to come to me as he did," he went on.

"Mr. Jardell?" asked Tom. "Who is he?"

"Why, the treasurer of the traction company."

"Then you haven't seen a man named Merrick and another named Pike?" asked Sam.

"Why, no. Who are they?"

"Two rascals who were up to some game. We think they were after your traction company bonds."

"Ha! perhaps—But no, that couldn't be," murmured Mr. Rover, wiping off the spectacles he wore. "I—er—I really do not understand this, boys."

"Tell us what you've been doing, uncle, and then we'll tell what we know," said Dick.

"Um! Well, you know that some time ago I invested in ten thousand dollars worth of traction company bonds—got them through an agent in New York."

"Yes."

"Well, about a week ago I received a private letter from Mr. Jardell, of the traction company, stating that there was something wrong with the bonds. Some plates had been stolen and counterfeit bonds printed."

"Yes."

"I was asked to keep quiet about the matter, for if the facts became generally known the public would become frightened and the bonds would go down in the stock market. Mr. Jardell said he would meet me at Carwell and have the printer look at my bonds and find out if they were genuine or not."

"And what did you do then?" asked Dick, who began to smell a mouse, as the saying goes.

"I sent Mr. Jardell word I would meet him at the Carwell hotel to-day. We met, and he and his printer, a man named Grimes, said the bonds I possessed were counterfeits."

"And then what?"

"Of course I was very much distressed," went on Randolph Rover, calmly. "I did not know what to do. But Mr. Jardell was very nice about it. He said he would take the bonds and get the company to issue good ones in their place. He gave me a receipt for them, and I am to have the good bonds next week."

"Why should he give you good bonds for bad ones?" said Tom, who, like Dick, was almost certain something was wrong.

"I asked that question, too, Thomas, but he said the reputation of his company was at stake. He did not want the public at large to know that bogus bonds were on the market."

"Uncle Randolph, do you know this Mr. Jardell personally?" asked Dick.

"Why—er—not exactly. But his letters—"

"How did he look?"

As well as he was able Mr. Rover described the man and also his companion. The boys exchanged glances.

"Merrick and Pike," muttered Tom.

"What is that you say, Thomas?"

"We think those men were swindlers," said Sam.

"Swindlers! Oh, my dear Samuel, impossible!" cried Randolph Rover aghast. "Why, they were very nice gentlemen, very nice. They asked me how my scientific farming was getting along, and both had read my article in the *Review* on the grafting of grape vines, and—"

"But we know these chaps," said Dick, "and they are called Merrick and Pike."

"And they talked about getting the best of you," added Tom. "That is why we followed you to Carwell. Where are the men now?"

"They have gone away. But—"

"Were they in a green runabout—an auto runabout?"

"They had a runabout, yes. I do not remember what color it was."

"The same fellows!" cried Dick. "Uncle Randolph, unless we are very much mistaken, you have been tricked, swindled! They have robbed you of the ten thousand dollars worth of bonds!"

Arthur M. Winfield

CHAPTER VI

WAITING FOR NEWS

It took Randolph Rover several minutes to comprehend the various statements made by the boys. That he had really been swindled by such nicely-spoken men as he had met at the Carwell hotel seemed extraordinary to him.

"I understand the bonds were not registered," said Dick.

"That is true," groaned his uncle.

"Then anybody could use them."

"Yes, although I have the numbers,—on a sheet in my desk at home."

"Well, that will make it more difficult for the rascals to dispose of them," said Sam.

"I'd like to catch that Merrick and that Pike, and punch their heads for them," commented Tom. It angered him exceedingly to see how readily his open-minded relative had fallen into the swindlers' trap.

"But there may be some mistake," said Randolph Rover, in a

forlorn tone. "Would that Merrick dare to impersonate Mr. Jardell?"

"Swindlers will do anything," answered Sam.

"We can make sure of that point by sending word to the traction company offices," answered Dick. "You are sure Mr. Jardell is the treasurer?"

"Yes—Mr. Andrew D. Jardell."

"Let us go back to town and see if we can catch him by long distance 'phone or by telegraph."

Shaking his head sadly, Randolph Rover turned his buggy around and followed the boys to the central office of the telephone company. Here all was activity on account of the broken-down wires, but communications were being gradually resumed. They looked into the telephone book, and at last got a connection which, a few minutes later, put them into communication with Andrew D. Jardell's private residence in the city.

"Is Mr. Jardell at home?" asked Dick, who was doing the telephoning.

"Mr. Jardell is away," was the answer.

"Is he at or near Carwell, New York state?"

"No, he is in Paris, and has been for two weeks."

"You are sure of this?"

"Yes."

"Who are you?"

"I am Mrs. Jardell. Who are you?"

"My name is Richard Rover. My uncle, Randolph Rover, has been swindled out of some traction company bonds by a man who said he was Mr. Jardell."

"Mercy me! You don't say so! Well, my husband had nothing to do with it, you may be sure. He went to London first and then to Paris, and in a day or two he is to start for Switzerland. His health is very poor and the doctor said he needed the trip."

Some more talk followed, and Mrs. Jardell advised Dick to communicate with the traction company at once, and he said he would do so.

"It wasn't Mr. Jardell at all, Uncle Randolph," said the youth, as he hung up the receiver. "The whole thing was a cleverly-planned swindle, and unless you can get the bonds back you'll be out the money."

At this announcement Mr. Rover nearly collapsed—for he was rather a retired man, and had had little to do in a business way since his trip to Africa with the boys, as related in "The Rover Boys in the Jungle." He did not know what to do, and stood rubbing his hands nervously.

"The swindlers!" he murmured. "Really, it is getting so that nobody can be trusted!"

"The best thing we can do is to send word to the various towns to stop the runabout with the two men in it on sight and have the rascals held by the authorities," said Dick, who felt he must take charge of affairs.

"That's the talk!" cried Tom, "and the sooner we get at it the better."

"Let us find out where that side road leads to," added Sam, "I mean the road on which we heard the auto."

Inside of an hour various messages had been sent by telephone and telegraph. It was now growing late and the Rovers hardly knew what to do next. From their uncle the boys got the whole tale concerning the bonds, but the new light shed on the subject did not help matters.

They also told the authorities about the cave and the boxes stored there, and some men were at once sent off to investigate and take possession of whatever could be found.

"I think some of us ought to go home," said Sam. "Aunt Martha won't go to bed until we get back, and she will be greatly worried."

It was finally decided that Tom and Dick should remain at the Carwell hotel over night and Sam and his uncle should go home in the buggy. The team was put up at the hotel barn, and then all hands went to the dining room for a late supper.

"I'm as hungry as two bears," announced Tom.

"Well, I shan't say no to a good feed," answered Sam.

Randolph Rover could eat but little. Now that he realized what had occurred, he upbraided himself bitterly for having been so deluded.

"They talked about scientific farming just to get me into good humor," he said, bitterly. "I see it all! Oh, if I can only get my hands on them!"

After Mr. Rover and Sam had departed, Dick and Tom wandered around the hotel and the vicinity for three hours. They anxiously awaited some message regarding the two swindlers, but nothing came. Then, worn out by the strenuous day they had put in, they went to bed and slept soundly until morning.

Before having breakfast they asked for messages. There was one from a village called Bahan, saying a green runabout with two men had passed through there about midnight. But the men had not been captured, and it was not known what had become of them.

At noon the telephone line between Oak Run and Carwell was in working order once more, and the boys sent word home. Then they left directions at the hotel, so that any messages coming in might be transmitted to the Rover farm.

"Well, I never!" cried Dick, suddenly.

"What now?" asked his brother.

"That freight thief, and that stuff in the cave—"

"Humph! it slipped my mind entirely. I was thinking only of Uncle Randolph's bonds."

"Let us find out if anything has been done."

At the local police headquarters they found that a wagon had just come in, loaded with the three full boxes of goods located at the cave. A search was still in progress for Dangler, but so far he had not been located.

"This clears up the mystery of the freight thefts," said an officer to the boys. "I only hope we can get our hands on

Bill Dangler."

"You know him?" asked Dick.

"Oh, yes. Years ago he used to work for the freight division of the railroad."

"Do you know anything of this Merrick and the fellow called Pike?"

"No, but our idea is that the three men were in the deal together. Probably this Merrick and this Pike pulled off this affair of the traction company bonds as a side issue."

"Have the freight robberies been large?" asked Sam.

"Not so large at one time, but they have been going on for months, and the total from four different stations along the line foots up to a good many thousand dollars."

"Well, I hope we catch all three of the men—and any others who may be in league with them," said Dick, and then he and Tom walked off. A little later they were on the buckboard and bound for home.

When they arrived at the farm they found that their uncle had sent a long letter to the officers of the traction company, relating in full what had occurred. In return the officials of the concern said they would put a private detective on the case, and this was done. But weeks went by and nothing was seen or heard of Merrick and Pike, and what had become of the missing bonds remained a mystery.

"I am anxious to take a look at that cave where the stolen freight was stored," said Sam one day. "Supposing we drive to it?"

"That will suit me," answered Dick. "I want to learn about something else—that red tin box I saw hanging from a tree."

"Oh, yes, I had forgotten about that," put in Tom. "Well, shall we walk or drive over?"

It was decided to drive as far as the cave, and not knowing how long they would be gone, the boys took a lunch along.

"Now, take care of yourselves," warned Randolph Rover. "Don't fall into any more holes."

"We'll try to watch out!" sang out Tom.

Then Dick cracked the whip, and off the team started at a good pace, the eldest Rover, however, holding them well under control. It was a clear and beautiful day. The boys did not dream of the odd adventure in store for them.

CHAPTER VII

A STRANGE LETTER BOX

"It won't be long now before we'll have to get back to Putnam Hall," observed Sam, as they drove along. "Dear old school! How I love it!"

"It's too bad that we are getting too old to go there," said Tom. "But we can't be boys always."

"I shall be glad to see the other fellows again," came from Dick.

"Do you know what I think?" declared Tom. "I think the Putnam Hall cadets are the finest lot of boys in the world!"

"Throwing bouquets at yourself, Tom?" said Sam, with a laugh.

"Well, don't you agree with me?"

"I certainly do, Sam, and Captain Putnam is the best teacher in the world. My, but won't we have fun when we get back!"

"We'll have to have a feast in honor of our return," said Dick, and smiled that quiet smile of his which meant so much.

Arthur M. Winfield

The distance to the cave was soon covered, and the boys tied their team to a tree in that vicinity. They went inside and found that everything, even to the empty boxes, had been taken away. The place had been explored by a number of curiosity seekers.

"It is queer that this cave wasn't discovered before," was Dick's comment, after they had spent half an hour in walking around.

"Perhaps the opening to the road wasn't so large formerly," suggested Tom. "Dangler may have enlarged it, so he could drive in."

"That is true. Well, it will be a regular picnic place after this. Its fame will spread for miles around." And Dick was right, and the cave is a well-known spot in that portion of New York state to this day.

The boys had brought with them two electric pocket lights, as they are called—lights they had purchased while on their river outing—and with these turned on they walked to the extreme rear of the cave and along the various passageways running up the mountainside.

"Here is where we dropped in," said Dick, pointing out the spot.

"I wish we could drop out—and land up on the mountain outside," returned his youngest brother. "Then, maybe, you could locate that tin lunch box, or whatever it was."

"I'd get up,
Very soon
If I had,
A big balloon!"

sang out Tom, merrily. "But as there doesn't seem to be a balloon handy, what's the matter with trying to climb up?" he added.

"And pull down several tons of dirt and rock on your head," said Dick. "Better go slow. We already know how treacherous these holes are. You'll get out of one by getting into another that's worse."

"I brought a lariat along," said Sam.

"A lariat?" queried the others.

"Sure,—the one I bought when we were out west. I thought we might use it for climbing purposes. It is light but strong, and we can lasso a tree or stump up there with it."

"Hurrah! Sam has solved the problem of how the Rover boys shall rise in the world!" exclaimed Tom, gaily. "Sam, try your skill by all means."

"Show me the tree or stump and I will," answered his brother readily.

As well as they were able, they crawled from one part of the hole to a spot that was somewhat higher. Then they found a projecting rock above them and Sam threw the noose of his lariat over this.

"Will it hold?" queried Dick. "You don't want to try to climb up and fall."

With caution Sam pulled on the lariat. It held, and he went up hand over hand, for he was a fair athlete. Then his brothers followed. They now stood on a ledge of rock, and the top of the hole was still twelve feet above them.

"There is a small tree, Sam," said Tom, looking upward. "If you can lasso that I think we'll be all right."

Once more the youngest Rover started to use the lariat. As it swung upward it missed the tree and swished out of sight over the edge of the hole.

"Ouch!" came the unexpected cry from above. "Oh, my eye!"

"Hullo! you've lashed somebody!" ejaculated Dick.

"I didn't know there was anybody up there," answered Sam, as the noose of the lasso slipped downward.

The three Rover boys looked upward. They heard a hasty movement in the bushes and caught a brief glimpse of a man's face. On the instant the man disappeared, muttering something to himself.

"It was Dangler!" ejaculated Dick.

"Are you sure?" asked both of the others, in a breath.

"Almost positive."

Dick had scarcely spoken the last words when down into the hole came a shower of dirt and stones, shoved over the edge above. The boys were struck by the stones and got some of the dirt in their eyes. Then down came a second mass of the same sort.

"Sto—stop that!" spluttered Tom, when he could speak. "Do you want to kill us?"

There was no answer, but down came more dirt and stones, until the boys were almost covered. What to do they did not know, until Dick suggested they drop from the ledge and seek safety in the cave. As they went down, a fair-sized rock followed, scraping Tom's shoulder and causing him to utter a sharp cry of pain.

"Are you hurt, Tom?" asked his two brothers.

"Oh, it isn't much," panted Tom. "But I wish I could get my hands on that rascal, that's all!"

"I am sure now that it must be Dangler," said Dick. "Nobody else around here would try to injure us. He is mad because we have exposed him. He must know the officers of the law are looking for him."

"I wish we could catch the rascal," muttered Tom.

"Supposing we climb the mountain from the outside?" suggested Sam. "It is a perfectly clear day and is early yet. We'll know enough to look out for pitfalls. If we can catch this Dangler the three of us ought to be able to manage him."

"If we are going to try anything like that we want to hurry," returned Dick. "He won't remain in this locality long—now he knows he is discovered."

"Maybe he thinks we didn't see him," came from Tom.

"Well, that will be in our favor. But he'll know somebody will be after him, for throwing down the dirt and stones."

Having eaten a hasty lunch and washed it down with water from a nearby spring, the three lads began the ascent of the mountain. This was hard work and caused them to perspire freely.

Arthur M. Winfield

"I'm glad I'm not fat," said Tom. "If I was I'd be winded sure."

"I think we'd better keep quiet as soon as we reach the vicinity of the holes," cautioned Dick.

Half an hour of hard climbing brought the boys to the vicinity where they had first fallen into the holes leading to the cave, and then they advanced cautiously and in almost absolute silence. They stopped to listen several times, but heard nothing but the calls of some birds and the trickling of water over the rocks.

Arriving at the top of the hole from where the dirt and stones had been thrown, they gazed around with interest. Where the soil was soft they could see the footprints of shoes much larger than those they themselves wore.

"Here is his trail, going away," said Dick, after a close examination.

"There is your tin box!" cried Sam, pointing to the object, still dangling from a distant tree.

"Wait till I see what is in it," answered his big brother. "It won't take but a minute or two."

"Beware of holes!" cautioned Tom.

Feeling his way through the brushwood, Dick approached the dangling tin box. It was a small affair and now hung open. He felt certain in his mind that when he had seen it before it had been closed.

The box proved to be empty and Dick was, somehow, disappointed. He glanced on the ground and saw a number of bits of paper, some old looking and some new. He picked up some of the bits and saw they had been written on in pencil, but the words or parts of words were undecipherable.

"Well, what do you make of it?" questioned Sam, as he and Tom came up.

"I think I know what this is," answered Dick.

"What?"

"A sort of a private post-office. Somebody was in the habit of leaving messages here, and Dangler or somebody else got the messages from time to time."

CHAPTER VIII

LAST DAYS ON THE FARM

"I believe you are right," said Tom, after he, too, had looked over some of the bits of paper strewn around. "Here is the word 'box' and here is the word 'Saturday.'"

"Yes, and here are the words, 'fast freight,'" added Sam. "This was nothing more than a letter box for the freight thieves."

"But why was it placed here?" questioned Dick. "It's a very out-of-the-way place and hard to get to."

"Maybe somebody had to come this way," answered Tom. "See, here is something of a trail."

"Yes, and here are those same big footprints!" exclaimed Sam. "For all we know they may lead to some house or hut on the mountainside."

Having picked up the majority of the bits of paper and put them in their pockets for future examination, the three Rover boys followed the path or trail they had discovered. It led along the mountainside to where there was a small clearing, backed up by a series of rocks from which a spring gushed forth, sparkling brightly in the sunshine.

"I'd like to get another drink," said Sam; "I am terribly thirsty to-day."

"Wait!" warned Dick, and caught his youngest brother by the arm.

"What's up, Dick?"

"I see a log cabin—over yonder, among the trees."

"Yes, and I see Dangler!" yelled Tom, suddenly. "There he goes, with a big bundle over his shoulder!" And he pointed to the rear of the log cabin. A man was just disappearing behind a fringe of brushwood. The bundle he carried appeared to be tied up in a horse blanket. He was running as hard as he could.

For a moment the boys did not know what to do. Then they ran to the cabin and entered. It contained but one room, and this they soon discovered was deserted. In the chimney a fire was smouldering, and the remains of a meal lay scattered over a box that did duty as a table.

"This must have been Dangler's hangout," was Dick's comment. "He must have come back for his things."

"Yes, and this explains why the queer letter box was stationned back there," said Tom.

"Aren't you going to try to catch him?" asked Sam, impatiently.

"To be sure," answered Dick, and rushed out, and the others after him.

"Keep back there!" they heard Dangler cry, as they appeared on the trail back of the log cabin. "Keep back, or it will be the worse for you!"

"Stop!" called Dick. "You might as well give up Dangler; you are bound to be caught some time."

"Not much! I am armed and I warn you to keep back," answered the freight thief, and then a bend of the trail hid him from view.

"Do you think he'd dare to shoot?" asked Tom.

"There is no telling what a desperate man will do," replied Dick. "We had better be cautious."

After that they advanced with care. Presently the trail came out on a mountain road and this passed over some rocks and crossed two other roads. They saw no more of Dangler, and the footprints had disappeared.

"He has slipped us," said Tom, coming to a halt and resting on a fallen tree. "Hang the luck anyway!"

"He came back to the cabin for his things," mused Sam. "I guess he is going to leave the neighborhood, and maybe for good."

Chagrined over their failure to catch the freight thief, the boys looked around that neighborhood for awhile and then retraced their steps to the log cabin. Here they found several old articles of wearing apparel and a few newspapers.

"Here is an envelope," said Sam, fishing the object out from behind the box that had done duty as a table. "It is addressed to William Dangler. Must have been some letter he got."

"Anything in it?"

"No."

"What is the postmark?"

"It is almost blurred out," said Sam. He took the envelope to the light. "Well, I declare! Ithaca!"

"Ithaca!" cried Tom.

"Why, that's the city we stop at to take the boat for Putnam Hall," exclaimed Dick.

"I know it."

"This is interesting, to say the least," was the comment of the oldest Rover boy. "Wonder if Dangler has friends or confederates in Ithaca?"

"We must notify the police of this," said Tom. "And the sooner the better."

Satisfied that they could learn nothing more by remaining around the log cabin, the boys departed, and inside of an hour were on their buckboard and bound for the farm. From that place they called up the authorities and informed them of what they had learned. Another search was at once instituted for Bill Dangler, but the rascal was not captured.

The next day Mr. Anderson Rover came home, and the boys and Randolph Rover had to acquaint him with all that had taken place. He shook his head when he heard of the unregistered bonds.

"I am afraid you will never see them again, Randolph," he

said to his brother.

"I am afraid so myself," was the mournful reply.

Anderson Rover had come home to see his boys off to school.

"I want you to make the most of your opportunities while at Putnam Hall this term," he said, "for it is to be your last."

"Yes, I know that," answered Tom. "But after that, what?"

"We will talk that over later, Tom. You must either go to college or get ready to go into business."

"I'd like to go to college!" put in Dick.

"So would I—if I knew what kind of a place it was," added Tom.

"If it was as fine a place as Putnam Hall I'd jump at it," came from Sam.

The next few days flew by quickly. During that time Dick received a letter from Dan Baxter, the former bully of Putnam Hall, which interested him not a little. This letter ran, in part, as follows:

"I am glad to say that I am now doing fairly well. I tried several positions and am now a traveling salesman for a large carpet house. I get fifteen dollars per week, all my expenses, and a commission on sales, so I consider myself lucky.

"When I look back on what I once was, Dick, I can scarcely realize what a change has come. But I feel happier than I ever was, and I am in hopes that I shall live to make a man of myself yet. I am trying to give up all my bad habits, and I haven't smoked, or drank a glass of liquor, since I left you in the south."

* * * * *

"That's the kind of a letter I like to get," said Dick, as he let his brothers peruse the communication. "It does a fellow's heart good, doesn't it?"

"I am glad we let him have that hundred dollars," said Sam. "Do you think he'll pay it back?"

"Here is a postscript in which he says he will send a money order next week."

"He certainly means to pull himself together," said Tom. "Well, now he has turned over a new leaf, I wish him the best of luck."

Almost before they knew it, it was time to leave the farm and journey to Putnam Hall. Everybody was sorry to see them go.

"I can't abide yo' boys being away nohow!" wailed Aleck Pop. "It jess don't seem natural to have yo' gone, dat's wot it don't!"

"Oh, we'll be back some day, Aleck," answered Dick. "And if we go off on some trip later, maybe we'll take you along."

"I most wish I was a waiter ag'in at de Hall," sighed the colored man.

"They can't spare you from here," said Sam.

Arthur M. Winfield

"Oh, I know dat, Sam."

The boys' trunks had been packed and sent on ahead, so all they carried with them were their dress-suit cases. Their father drove them to the railroad station at Oak Run, and their aunt and uncle and the others around the farm came out on the piazza to see them off.

"Now be good boys," admonished their Aunt Martha. "And take care and don't get sick."

"And be sure and study all you can," said their Uncle Randolph. "Remember nothing is quite so grand as learning in this world."

"Yo' keep out ob mischief!" cried Aleck Pop, shaking a warning finger at Tom, who grinned broadly.

And then the carriage started off, and the journey to Putnam Hall was begun.

CHAPTER IX

AT THE WILD WEST SHOW

As my old readers know, Putnam Hall was located not far from the village of Cedarville on Cayuga Lake. To get to the school the boys had to take a train to Ithaca and then board a little lake steamer stopping at Cedarville and various other points along the shore.

"It seems a long time since we were at the Hall," observed Dick, as they settled down in the train.

"And what a lot of things have happened since then!" exclaimed Sam. "I can tell you what, we'll have a story to tell to the others, won't we?"

"I guess Songbird, Fred, and Hans Mueller have already told everything," returned Tom. "More than likely Songbird has concocted some verses about it."

The run to Ithaca took several hours, and they lunched at noon in the dining car. It was a beautiful day, and the boys enjoyed the scenery as much as if they had never seen it before.

"I hope we can make a good connection for Cedarville," said

Sam as they left the train and started for the dock from which the *Golden Star* made her trips on the lake. But they were doomed to disappointment, the steamboat had had a break-down and would be delayed two hours or more.

As there was nothing to do but to wait, the boys checked their dress-suit cases and then started for a stroll through the city. They soon learned that a wild west show was giving an exhibition there and consequently the place was crowded with folks from the surrounding districts.

"I shouldn't mind going to the wild west show," observed Tom. "Do you think we have time?"

"We could spend an hour there anyway," answered Sam.

"It depends on where the show is to be held," came from Dick.

They soon ascertained that the show grounds were not far off, and made their way thither. The exhibition had already started, and they got inside the big tent-like enclosure as speedily as possible.

The show was a fairly good one, and the boys thoroughly enjoyed the trick riding by cowboys, and the fancy rifle shooting. Then came some wild riding by real Indians.

"Almost makes a fellow feel as if he'd like to be on a horse himself," said Tom. He liked horseback riding very well.

"Say, I want you to look over there," said Sam, pointing to the seats some distance away. "Do you see that man sitting near the bottom—right beside that boy with the basket of peanuts?"

Tom and Dick looked in the direction pointed out, and the eldest Rover gave a start.

"Sam, do you think it is the fellow called Merrick?" he exclaimed.

"Doesn't he look like it?"

"He certainly does—now you speak of it," came from Tom. "And, by the way, don't you remember about that envelope picked up in the log cabin? It was postmarked Ithaca."

"So it was! Perhaps this Merrick lives here."

"Let us go over and get a closer look at him," said Dick, and left his seat, followed by the others.

There was a large crowd, so they had some difficulty in making their way to where the man was located. In his haste, Dick bumped against a waiter selling lemonade and spilled the contents of two glasses on the ground.

"Excuse me," he said.

"Hi! you've got to pay for the lemonade," roared the waiter, angrily. "You pay up, you clumsy clown!"

"See here, my man, I'll pay you, but I want you to understand you can't call me a clown," said Dick, angrily.

"Ah! go on wid yer! Pay up, see?"

"Here's your money," and Dick held out ten cents. "Now, am I a clown or not?"

"Well, er—"

Arthur M. Winfield

"Am I or not?" And the eldest Rover boy doubled up his fists. He knew he must "take the bull by the horns" with such an individual as that before him.

"Excuse me," mumbled the fellow and moved away. "I—er—suppose yer couldn't help it."

Sam and Tom had gone ahead and they were now close to the man they took to be Merrick.

"No mistake here!" declared Sam, as he got a good, square look at the fellow's face.

"He sees us!" exclaimed Tom, a second later. "He is trying to get away."

The boy was right, Merrick had seen them. He was greatly amazed, for he had not dreamed of their being in that vicinity. He left his seat in a hurry, and, elbowing his way through the crowd, started for the entrance to the big tent-like enclosure.

By this time Dick was coming up and Sam and Tom quickly acquainted him with what was going on. All three of the Rovers pushed through the big crowd after Merrick, but, before they could draw near, the rascal was outside and running between a number of carriages and wagons standing in that vicinity.

"Come on after him!" cried Tom. "We must capture him if we can!"

They set off on a smart run, but Merrick could run also, and fear now lent speed to his flying feet. On and on went the swindler, with the Rover boys less than a square behind him. Then, as they came to a number of tall buildings, Merrick darted around a corner and out of sight.

When the Rover boys reached the corner they looked in every direction for the man. Only a few people were about, the majority of the town folks being at the show.

"Wonder if he went straight on, or took to some side street?" mused Dick.

"I'll go straight on," said Sam. "Dick, you can take one side street and Tom can take the other," and away went the youngest Rover, at a fresh burst of speed.

Sam's advice was considered good, and soon all of the boys had scattered. The street Tom followed was lined with tall tenements and ended in little more than an alleyway.

Coming to another corner, Tom paused and gazed in all directions. As he turned his head he saw a man look out from a tenement doorway. Then the head was drawn back quickly.

"Merrick!" muttered Tom to himself, and turned back to the tenement, which was a building four stories high. On one side was something of an alleyway and beyond were other tenements, and the rear of a big building used for a factory and offices.

Tom found the front door of the tenement wide open and he did not hesitate to go in. Nobody was in sight, but he heard hasty footsteps on the floor above.

"Merrick! you might as well give up!" he called out. "Come down here!"

"Go on about your business, young fellow!" came the reply. "If you try to follow me you'll get the worst of it."

Undaunted by this threat, Tom mounted the stairs two steps at a time. As he did so he heard Merrick go up a second flight and then a third.

"Must think he can hide on the roof," thought Tom. "Well, I'll corner him if I can."

As Tom ran through the hallway on the third floor a door opened and an old woman confronted him.

"What do yez want here?" she demanded, in strong Irish accents.

"I am after a thief," answered Tom.

"A thafe! Sure an' there's no thafe in this house."

"He just ran in here from the street."

"Bedad, is that true now? Where did he go to?"

"I don't know. How do you get to the roof?"

"Be the laddher at the back av the hall."

The old woman pointed in the direction, and Tom sped on. Soon he reached a common wooden ladder leading to a scuttle, which was wide open. As the youth mounted the ladder the scuttle was banged shut, almost hitting him on the top of the head. Then he heard hasty footsteps across the roof.

"Maybe he thinks he can jump to one of the other buildings," said Tom to himself. "Well, if he can do it, so can I."

He pushed the scuttle up with difficulty, for it was heavy.

Then with caution, for he did not want to receive a kick in the head, he gazed around the roof of the tenement. Nobody was in sight.

With caution Tom stepped out on the roof. A number of chimneys were not far off, and he wondered if Merrick was concealed behind them.

"I wish I had a club or something," he thought. "I'd have a tough time of it up here, if it came to a hand-to-hand struggle."

With eyes on the alert, Tom made his way to one chimney and then another. The swindler was not there, nor was he on the adjoining roof. Then the youth got down on his hands and knees and looked over the edge of the tenement, on the alleyway side. Here was an iron fire escape, running from the fourth story to the second. On the fire escape he saw Merrick, descending to the bottom with all possible rapidity.

CHAPTER X

JOLLY OLD SCHOOLMATES

Evidently the swindler had dropped from the roof to the upper landing of the fire escape. He was now almost to the bottom.

"Stop!" cried Tom, but he knew the command was a useless one. At the sound of his voice Merrick looked up and muttered something the boy could not catch. Then he swung himself from the bottom landing of the fire escape and dropped to the ground.

"If he can get down that way, so can I," thought Tom, and in another moment he was descending the escape in the same fashion as the swindler had done. As he reached the second landing of the escape he saw Merrick turn the corner of the alleyway and disappear on the street beyond.

When Tom came out on the street he almost ran into the arms of two burly men who had come out of the tenement. Both caught him by the arms.

"What does this mean, young fellow?" asked one, savagely. "Doing the sneak-thief act?"

"I am after a thief," was the answer. "Did you see a man running away?"

"No, and we don't think there was a man," answered one of the tenement dwellers.

"Well, there was a man," said Tom. "Come, if you will help me catch him I will reward you well."

"What did he steal?"

"Some bonds worth ten thousand dollars—they belonged to my uncle," explained Tom, hastily.

The promise of a reward made the men attentive and they soon agreed to assist Tom as much as possible. Then Dick and Sam came in sight, and had to be told of what had happened.

The two men knew the tenement and factory district well, and they led in a hunt lasting over half an hour, and a policeman was likewise called into service.

"I've heard of that bond case," said the policeman. "I'd like to lay my hands on Merrick."

But the hunt was a useless one, for Merrick could not be found. For their trouble Tom gave the two men from the tenement a dollar each, with which they had to be satisfied. The policeman promised to report the matter at headquarters, and as there seemed to be nothing else to do, the three Rover boys walked down to the steamboat dock, first, however, sending a telegram to Randolph Rover, relating briefly what had occurred.

"It's a great pity we didn't catch this Merrick," sighed Tom,

Arthur M. Winfield

when they were steaming along the lake shore. "Perhaps we'll never see or hear of him again."

"Well, we don't want Merrick as much as we want Uncle Randolph's traction company bonds," answered Dick. "If he has disposed of the bonds it won't do much good to catch him,—unless, of course, he can get the bonds back."

"And he may not have had the bonds," put in Sam. "That fellow Pike may have handled them."

"That is true, too,—although I somehow think Merrick is the prime mover in this swindle."

"I think that, too," said Tom.

The *Golden Star* was a trim little side-wheeler with a fair-sized deck fore and aft. The boys sat on the forward deck, and as the boat ran along the shore of the lake they pointed out many localities known to them.

"There is where we went on the paper chase," said Sam.

"Yes, and that is where we went on one of the encampments," added Tom.

"We came fishing down here once," put in Dick. "One of the boys went overboard."

"It was John Fenwick, the fellow we used to call Mumps," said Tom. "By the way, I wonder what has become of him?"

"Went west, I think," answered Sam. "One of the boys said he was in the insurance business with some relative."

"He was a great toady to Dan Baxter."

"So he was, but he had some good points, too."

So the talk ran on, until Cedarville was reached. On account of the delay it was dark, and the boys wondered if they would find any conveyance to take them to the Hall.

"Hullo, here is Peleg Snuggers with the carryall!" cried Sam, as the general utility man of the school appeared. "How are you, Peleg?"

"Fust rate," replied the man, grinning. "Been waiting a long time for you."

"Sorry, but we couldn't make the captain hurry the boat," answered Dick.

"Peleg, you're a sight for tired optics," said Tom, giving the man's hand a squeeze that made him wince. "How's your grandmother?"

"Why, Master Tom, I ain't—"

"And your great-granduncle? Is he over the shingles yet?"

"Why, Master Tom, I ain't got no—"

"And your second cousin by your first wife's sister? Did she get over the heart failure she had when the canary took a fit?"

"Now, see here, Master Tom, don't you go for to joking an old man—"

"Joking, Peleg?" returned Tom, solemnly. "Why, you know I never joke." And he took on an injured look.

"Don't joke, eh? Well, if you ain't the greatest joker Putnam Hall ever see then I'll eat my hat," declared Peleg. "Jump in an' don't ask me about no grandfathers, or wife's sisters, nor nuthing. Ain't you hungry?"

"Hungry? I could eat a brickbat fried in lemon oil."

"Then, unless you hurry, you won't get no supper."

"Oh, Mrs. Green will get something for us, never fear," said Dick, mentioning the matron of Putnam Hall, who was a warm-hearted and generous woman, even though a little bit "peppery" at times.

"All the other boys here now?" asked Dick, as they drove off in the direction of Putnam Hall.

"I reckon the most of 'em are, Master Dick. So many coming an' going I can hardly keep track of 'em."

"Fred Garrison, Songbird Powell and Hans Mueller back?" asked Sam.

"Yes, an' they told me some wonderful stories of your doings down south."

"Are Larry Colby and George Granbury here?" questioned Dick.

"Yes."

"I'll be glad to meet Larry and George again," went on Dick. "I suppose they'll have something to tell of what they did during vacation."

"Every time I come to the Hall I think of the first time I

came," said Tom. "Do you remember how I set off that giant firecracker?"

"Yes, and how old Josiah Crabtree put you under arrest for it," added Sam. "Wonder where old Crabtree is now?"

"He is out of prison," answered Peleg Snuggers. "I got that from a man in Cedarville. The man said as how Crabtree went to Canada."

"Hope he stays there and never attempts to bother Mrs. Stanhope again," was Dick's comment.

About half the distance to the Hall had been covered when there came a shout on the road and Peleg Snuggers had to rein in his team. Then several boys appeared, dressed in cadet uniforms, for Putnam Hall was a military academy.

"Whoop! here they are, fellows! Hurrah for the Rovers!"

"Rovers by name and rovers by nature!"

"Say, Tom, how do you like being adrift on the Gulf of Mexico?"

"Sam, don't you want to become a regular cowboy?"

"Dick, when I buy a houseboat I'm going to engage you as captain."

And then the students in the road clambered into the carryall and tumbled all over the Rovers, hugging them and trying to shake hands at the same time.

"Larry, glad to see you, but please don't smother me."

Arthur M. Winfield

"I'll love you, George, if only you won't put your elbow through my ribs."

"I knew Fred would meet us."

"You gif me der honor of dis," came from Hans Mueller. "I tole dem fellers to come along alretty."

"Good for you, Hansy, old boy!" cried Sam, and gave the German cadet a tight squeeze.

"Songbird, why don't you turn on the poetry pipe line and let her flow?" queried Larry Colby, who, even though an officer of one of the companies, was as jolly as the rest of the students.

"Yes, give us something by all means," said Tom. "Something about 'stilly night,' 'fond recollections,' 'starved cats,' and the like."

"Humph! 'stilly night' and 'starved cats'!" snorted Songbird Powell. "You must think I'm running a hash mill instead of—"

"By no means, Songbird, dear!" piped Tom. "We all know you're the sole owner of the largest poem factory in New York state. Let her flow by all means."

"If you don't recite, we'll sing," said Dick.

"No, don't do that—yet," pleaded Songbird. "I've got a verse or two all ready," and he began, in slow, measured tones:

"Back to dear old Putnam Hall!
Back to the days of yore!
Back to the good old times we had!

May we have many more!
Back to our lessons and our books,
And to the teachers, too,
Back to the drills and hours off—"

"And to the mutton stew!"

finished Tom. "Don't forget to put in Mrs. Green's wonderful mutton stews."

"No mutton stews in this!" snorted Songbird. "The last line was, 'When days were bright and blue,'" and then he continued:

"We love to gather here again,
And talk of times to come,
And plot and plan, and plan and plot—
And plan and plot—and plot and plot—
And plan—and plan—and plan—"

"Songbird, you've plotted and planned too much," interrupted Dick, as the would-be poet hesitated. "Let's sing a song."

"That's the talk!" cried Fred Garrison, and started up the song well known to all of them:

"Putnam Hall's the place for me!
Tra la lee! Tra la lee!
Putnam Hall's the place for me!
The best old school I know!"

And then, as the carryall swung up to the campus, they set up the school yell, which brought out a score of students to witness the arrival of the Rover boys.

CHAPTER XI

WILLIAM PHILANDER TUBBS

As my old readers know, Putnam Hall was a handsome structure of brick and stone standing in the center of a large plot of ground, bounded on two sides by cedar woods. To the front was the campus and the wagon road and beyond this a slope leading to the lake. To the rear were rich farm lands, cultivated solely for the benefit of the institution. Besides the school, there were a building fitted up as a gymnasium, and also several barns and carriage houses. The Hall was built in the form of the letter E, and was three stories high. It contained numerous classrooms, a private office, a large mess hall, or dining room, and both large and small dormitories.

The master of the school was Captain Victor Putnam, who was a bachelor, and as kind as he was strict. Captain Putnam was a West Point graduate, and had modeled his school somewhat after that famous government institution. When the school was first organized the Rover boys did not go there, but a number of other bright and lively lads did, and what these cadets accomplished has already been related in a line of stories called "The Putnam Hall Series," starting with "The Putnam Hall Cadets." These lads had some awful quarrels with the head assistant, Josiah Crabtree, and they were glad when the Rovers appeared and made it so hot for Crabtree that he had to leave. George Strong was now first assistant in place of Crabtree, and the cadets found him a teacher after their own heart.

"Hurrah! here are the Rovers!" was the cry from the campus. "Welcome back!"

"Boys, I am glad to see you again," came from Captain Putnam, as he appeared at the front door and shook hands. "From what I have heard you have had rather strenuous times during the past vacation."

"That is true, Captain," answered Dick. "I am glad to get back here."

"So am I glad," came from Tom and Sam, and all shook hands. Then the boys were told to go to the mess hall, where a hot supper awaited them. Here Mrs. Green met them with her round, ruddy and smiling face.

"It's wonderful stories I've heard of you," said the matron. "I declare, you'll have to go into a museum!"

"Not until after supper anyhow," answered Tom, dryly. And then everybody present laughed.

The supper over, the boys went up to their dormitory, and here as many of the cadets as could crowded in, to talk over the doings of the past vacation. Larry Colby had spent the time on the coast of Maine, and George Granbury had been to the Thousand Islands and to Montreal.

"Yes, Crabtree is in Canada," said George. "I met him in Montreal, and I can tell you, he looked seedy enough."

"Well, he deserves to be seedy," was Dick's comment. He could not forget how the former teacher had endeavored to hypnotize the widow Stanhope into marrying him, so that he could gain possession of the money she was holding in trust for Dora.

Of course all the boys wanted to know about Dan Baxter, for he had been a leading character at the Hall for many years. Some shook their heads at the idea of the former bully reforming.

"It will be the greatest surprise I ever heard of," was Larry's comment.

"He'll do it—mark my words," said Dick.

"Let us hope so," said George.

"Well, it would seem that Putnam Hall is not to suffer for the want of a bully," came from Fred. "We've got a new one here who is as bad as Dan Baxter ever was."

"Who is he?" questioned Dick, with interest.

"A chap named Tad Sobber. He is a big, overbearing fellow with hardly any education, and he wants to rule everybody. I can't understand how Captain Putnam took him as a pupil."

"He came well recommended, that's why," answered Songbird. "But I guess the captain has found out that the recommendation was false."

"He shan't rule me," said Tom, decidedly.

"We want no bullies here," put in Dick. "The day for all such is past."

"So say we all of us!" cried several cadets.

At that moment came a knock on the door, and a tall youth, wearing an unusually high collar and very large cuffs, came in.

"Well, if it isn't our old chum, William Philander Tubbs!" cried Dick, running forward and grasping the hand of the dude student.

"Hullo, Tubbsey, old man!" said Tom, gaily. "What's the price of the best cologne now?"

"Very—ah—glad to meet you again," drawled Tubbs. "But—er—please don't call me Tubbsey, because it isn't my name, don't you know."

"To be sure, Buttertub—I mean Washtub," answered Tom. "Had your hair crimped lately?"

"Now, Tom, I never crimp my hair—it hurts the color, don't you know," explained William Philander. "I use—"

"Glue with an egg beater," finished Tom with a wink at his friends. "By the way, Tubblets, do you know what I heard some girls say last week? They said they thought you were a regular fashion plate."

"Now did they really?" gushed the dude, much pleased. "Who—er—said it?"

"Two girls living not many miles from here."

"You—ah—don't happen to know their names?"

"No. But I can tell you all about them."

"Ah! Then please do, Tom," said the dude eagerly. To have any young ladies think of him pleased him immensely.

"Well, these are a couple of young ladies who work in a laundry. Maybe they wash your shirts. They are colored, and—"

"Colored!" gasped the dude, and then a shout of laughter went up, in the midst of which William Philander started to leave the room.

"Don't go away mad, Billy," cried Tom. "Isn't it nice even to have two dusky damsels think of you?"

"No, it is not—it is—is horrid!" answered William Philander. "I think you are—er—poking fun at me."

"Never did such a thing in my life, my dear fellow—it's against my internal regulations. But how have you been since the week before next month?"

"I had a delightful vacation."

"Took the girls out to ice-cream sociables and yellow teas every day you wasn't playing golf or hop-scotch, I suppose."

"I—er—took the young ladies out some—we had glorious times, don't you know. One moonlight night on Lake George I shall never forget, don't you know. We were out in a tiny rowboat and the moon was sparkling over the water, and Geraldine and I—"

"Lucky Geraldine!" sighed Tom. "And thrice lucky Philander Willander—I mean William Philander!"

"Can't you make up a poem about Geraldine, Songbird?"

asked Sam.

"And don't forget to put in the moonlight," came from Dick.

"And the silvery waves, and murmuring breeze," added Fred.

"How much older than you is Geraldine, any how?" quizzed Tom.

"Geraldine is—"

"You haven't got to tell her age if she is over thirty, Billy," said Larry. "Her age is sacred after that, you know."

"And don't tell us even if she has false teeth," came from Sam.

"And it doesn't make any real difference whether her hair is her own or not."

"It's hers if it is paid for," said Tom. "You don't suppose a girl that Billy would fall in love with would wear tresses that were stolen?"

"And to think she may be fat!" sighed Sam. "I hope she doesn't weigh over two hundred, Willy."

"Oh dear me!" cried the dude, in desperation. "I want you to remember—"

"That she is yours and yours only," finished Tom. "Yes, nobody shall walk in your corn patch, Bill—not over my dead body. But tell us—secretly if you must—does she wear a number eight shoe or a twelve?"

"If you don't stop your fooling—" gasped the dude.

Arthur M. Winfield

"He is going to keep his dreadful secrets to himself," cried Tom, mournfully. "Alack! and too bad! But never mind, we'll all come to the wedding, Tubblets, and bring lemons if you say so?"

"Who said I was going to get married?"

"Is it to be a church affair or just a little private home gathering?" went on Tom, seriously. "If it's to be in a church, and you want us all for rushers—I mean ushers, why—"

"We'll all be on the job," finished Dick. "Wouldn't miss the chance for a farm with a blind mule thrown in."

"Vots der madder mid me peing a flower girl?" asked Hans, grinning broadly.

"No, Hansy, you'll have to carry Billy's coat-tails for him," said Fred. "The latest style from London, don't you know, is to have them trailing on behind like—"

"Oh, stop! stop!" screamed William Philander, putting his hands to his ears. "You are all perfectly horrid, don't you know! I'll not remain another minute!" and he fled from the dormitory, the laughter of the crowd ringing in his ears as he departed.

CHAPTER XII

WHAT HAPPENED ON THE STAIRS

In a few days the Rover boys felt perfectly at home once more—indeed it was as if they had never been away, so Sam said. The majority of the students were old friends, although there was a fair sprinkling of new boys.

It was not until the end of the week that Dick Rover came into contact with Tad Sobber, a stocky youth, with a shock of black hair and eyes which were cold and penetrating. Sobber was with a chum named Nick Pell, and both eyed Dick in a calculating manner which was highly offensive.

"He's the fellow who does the hero act," whispered Sobber to Pell, in a manner meant to reach Dick's ears. "Wants to make a regular grand-stand play all the time."

Without hesitation Dick wheeled about.

"Was that remark intended for me?" he demanded, sharply.

His suddenness took Tad Sobber off his guard.

"What if it was?" he demanded in return.

"I don't like it, that's all."

"Humph! I don't care whether you like it or not," grunted Sobber.

"See here, Tad Sobber, let us have an understanding," said Dick, calmly. "I understand that you are trying to bully everybody in this school. Now, this cannot be. We have had several bullies here and we have gotten rid of them all. We want no more."

"Humph! Trying to be the bully yourself, eh?" sneered Sobber.

"No, I am only giving you warning. The other boys have told me about you."

"Tad has a right to act as he pleases," put in Nick Pell.

"No, he has not. Captain Putnam expects every student here to be a gentleman."

"Oh, don't preach, Rover," cried Tad Sobber. "I can take care of myself without your advice."

"Well, I warn you to keep your distance so far as I am concerned and keep a civil tongue in your head," said Dick.

What this war of words might have led to there is no telling. Just at that moment the school bell rang, and all of the students had to hurry to their respective classes.

It may be mentioned here that Sam, Tom and Dick were now in the same grade. This may be wondered at, but the fact of the matter was that Sam, by hard work the term previous, had caught up to Tom, while Dick, because of being away on some business for his father at various times, had dropped a little behind.

"Had a little run-in with Sobber," said Dick to his brothers, when he got the chance, and related the particulars.

"He said something about me behind my back," said Sam. "I don't know what it was, but I am certain it was nothing complimentary."

"We must watch him," said Tom. "If we do not, he may try to play us foul."

As this was to be their last term at Putnam Hall, all of the Rovers determined to do their best in their studies, so they spent no time in fooling while at their classes. Once or twice Tom found it hard to resist playing a joke, but a look from Dick usually made him turn to his books again.

It was now the season for football, and several school teams had been organized. Tom and Dick were on one team, headed by Larry Colby. There was another team headed by Tad Sobber, and on this Nick Pell was a quarterback. How Sobber had ever gotten the captaincy of this team was a mystery.

"They want to play us next Saturday," said Larry, one afternoon. "What do you fellows say?" He put the question to his fellow members of the eleven.

"I don't care much to play Sobber and Pell," said Tom, promptly.

"Exactly the way I feel about it," added Dick. "But I'll play if the rest want to."

Some demurred, but in the end the match was arranged, and it started on the school grounds at two o'clock the following Saturday afternoon.

"I think it will be useless to try any mass playing," said Larry. "Sobber and Pell and some of the others are too heavy for us. We'll have to trust to some swift passes and quick runs."

In the first half of the game Sobber's eleven got ten points, while Larry's team got nothing.

"Sobber is too brutal for me," said Tom. "He deliberately kicked me in the shins."

"If he does it again, knock him down," advised Dick, promptly.

Larry's eleven went into the second half with vigor. They soon got a goal and followed it up by two more. Then Sobber claimed a foul, but it was not granted.

"If anybody is fouling it is you," said Dick. "You fouled Tom twice. If you do it again—"

"Never mind, Dick," interrupted Larry. "Go on and play, or give up," he added to Tad Sobber.

"I want Dick Rover to understand that he—" began Sobber, when another player pulled him back. Some hot words followed, and then the game proceeded. Larry's eleven made another touchdown and kicked the goal,—and thus won a substantial victory, much to Sobber's disgust and that of his crony, Nick Pell.

"No use of talking, those Rover boys make me sick," said

Sobber, when he and Nick Pell were alone. "Everybody in this school seems to toady to them."

"If I had been you I'd have pitched into Dick Rover on the gridiron," answered Pell.

"Well, I wanted to, but the others wouldn't have it. But I'll polish him off some day—and polish off Tom, too," added Sobber, uglily.

Two of the small boys of the school had been taken sick, and in order to keep them quiet they were removed to the top floor of the institution, and one of the colored waiters was ordered to carry their meals up to them. Dick knew both of the lads, and he frequently went up to pay them a visit and cheer them up a bit.

One day he was just returning from a visit to the sick students when he heard a noise in the hallway on the second floor. He looked down the stairs and saw Tom and Tad Sobber near a landing, having a wordy quarrel. Nick Pell was approaching and so were Fred and Hans.

"For two pins I'd give you a good thrashing, Rover," the bully was saying. "You can't lord it over me, understand that."

"Well, I want you to keep your distance, Tad Sobber," returned Tom. "And I stick to it that you kicked me on pur- pose during the football game."

Both boys were walking to the stairs landing, and Dick and the others who heard the words followed. Then of a sudden the crowd that was gathered saw Sobber catch Tom by the throat.

"Le—let go!" gasped Tom.

"Take that!" retorted the bully, and banged Tom's head against the wall.

There was a scuffle near the stairs, and both boys fell up against the railing.

"Look out, Tom!" cried Dick. "He'll throw you down the stairs!" And he tried to go to his brother's assistance. But before he could reach the spot the two contestants had separated.

"That for you!" roared Sobber, and aimed a blow for Tom's eye. Tom dodged, and then let out with his right fist. The blow landed on the bully's chin. He tottered backward, lost his balance, and pitched down the stairs.

Just as the bully went backwards, a side door of the mess hall opened and the colored waiter who carried the food to the sick lads upstairs came out. He held a trayful of dainties in his hands. Crash! came Sobber into the tray, and he and the dishes and the waiter went to the floor in a confused heap.

"Fo' de lan' sake!" gasped the waiter. "What fo' you dun dat to me?"

"Oh!" groaned the bully, and tried to get up. On one cheek he had a dab of jelly and his hand and shirt front were covered with broth. The sight was such a comical one that the boys on the landing could not help but laugh.

"Yo' dun bust de whole dinnah up!" was the waiter's comment, as he arose and surveyed the wreck. The food had been scattered in all directions and half of the dishes were broken.

"It wasn't my fault!" growled Tad Sobber. "Tom Rover knocked me down the stairs."

"It was your own fault," cried Tom. "You started the fight, I didn't."

"Somebody's got to pay fo' dis smash," said the waiter. "I ain't gwine to do it. Why, I ought to sue yo' fo' damages, dat's wot!" he added, glaring wrathfully at Sobber.

"I'll fix Tom Rover for this!" exclaimed the bully, and looked up the stairs at the laughing students. "I'll make him laugh on the other side of his face!"

And he ran up the stairs with the intention of attacking Tom again.

CHAPTER XIII

DORA, GRACE AND NELLIE

That Tad Sobber was in a thorough rage was easily to be seen. His eyes were full of hate and he looked ready to fly at Tom and tear him to pieces.

All of the boys expected to see a great fight, and some backed away from the landing, to give the contestants more room.

But before anything could be done Dick leaped to the front and barred the bully's further progress.

"Stop it, Sobber," he said quietly but firmly.

"Get out of my way, Dick Rover!" roared the bully. "This is none of your affair."

"Then I'll make it my affair," answered the eldest Rover boy. "You shall not attack my brother here."

"Don't worry, Dick—I can take care of him," put in Tom, undauntedly, and doubled up his fists. "Maybe he'd like to go down stairs again and smash some more dishes."

"Not when John Fly am carryin' dem," put in the colored waiter, who stood looking at the wreckage with a sober face. "I don't want no moah such knockovers, I don't!" And he shook his woolly head decidedly.

The noise had summoned numerous cadets to the scene, and now George Strong, the head teacher, appeared.

"What is the trouble here?" he demanded.

For the moment nobody answered him, and he gazed in wonderment at the broken dishes and the scattered food.

"Been a accident, sah," said John Fly. "Dat young gen'man dun fall down de stairs an' knock me ober, tray an' all, sah."

"Did you fall down stairs, Sobber?"

"No, sir, I was thrown down by Tom Rover," replied the bully.

"Thrown down?" repeated the head teacher in surprise.

"He attacked me and I hit back," explained Tom. "It was his own fault that he fell down stairs. Had he let me alone there would have been no trouble."

"It is false—he hit me first," said the bully.

"That is not so," cried Fred. "Sobber struck the first blow."

"Yah, dot is der fact alretty," put in Hans. "He vos caught Dom py der throat und knock his head py der vall chust so hard like nefer vos!"

"He hit me first, didn't he, Nick?" said the bully, turning to

Arthur M. Winfield

his crony.

"I—I think he did," stammered Nick Pell. He did not dare to tell an outright falsehood. "I think it was all Tom Rover's fault," he added, after a surly look from Sobber.

"All of you know it is against the rules to fight in this school," said Mr. Strong, sternly.

"Well, I only fought after I was attacked," answered Tom, doggedly.

"Mr. Strong, whether you believe it or not, my brother speaks the plain truth," came from Dick. "I was coming from Larmore's room and saw it all. Had you been in Tom's place you would have done as he did."

These plain words from Dick made George Strong hesitate. He knew the Rover boys well, and knew that they were generally in the right. More than this, he had caught Tad Sobber in a falsehood only the day before.

"You may all go to your rooms and I will see about this later," he said. "Sobber, as you broke the dishes, you will have to pay for them."

"Can't Rover pay half the bill?" growled the bully.

"No, for I cannot see how he is to blame for that."

After this some sharp words followed. Tad Sobber was impudent, and as a consequence was marched off to a storeroom which was occasionally used as a "guardhouse" by the teachers and Captain Putnam. Here he had to stay in solitary confinement for twenty-four hours and on the plainest kind of a diet. This imprisonment made Sobber furious, and he vowed he would get square with Tom and Dick for it if it cost him his life.

"They may have been able to down other fellows in this school, but they shan't down me," was what he told Nick Pell.

"Well, you want to go slow in what you do," answered Pell. "I've been talking to some of the others and I've learned that they got the best of several fellows who were here at different times—Dan Baxter, Lew Flapp and some others."

"Humph! I am not afraid of them," growled Tad Sobber. "I suppose they think, because they are rich and have traveled some, they can lord it over everybody. Well, I'll show them a trick or two before I'm done with them."

After Tad Sobber came out of confinement the Rover boys thought he might try to play some underhand trick on Tom, and consequently kept their eyes open. But nothing developed for some days, and then it came in a most unexpected way.

The boys settled down to their studies, but it was not in their nature to go in for all work and no play. On the following Saturday they asked for permission to visit Cedarville, to buy some things Sam and Tom needed. They took with them Songbird and Hans, and went on foot, the weather being ideal for walking. Just before leaving they saw Sobber and Pell hurry away, also in the direction of the town.

"I wonder where they are going?" mused Dick.

"Sobber is going to take a run by steamboat to Ithaca," answered Songbird. "I heard him speak to Captain Putnam about it."

"Is Pell going along?"

"I don't think so."

The three Rover boys and their friends were soon on the way. They felt in the best of spirits, and Powell could not resist the temptation to break out into his usual doggerel:

"I love to roam o'er hill and dale,
In calm or storm or windy gale,
I love the valley and the hill,
The brooklet and the running rill,
I love the broad and placid lake—"

"Where we can swim or take a skate,"

finished Tom, and then went on:

"And just remember, of the rest,
I love old Putnam Hall the best!"

"That last sentiment hits me," said Fred.
"Tell you what, fellows, no place like our school."

"I dink I make me some boetry alretty," said Hans, solemnly, and began:

"I lof to hear der insects hum,
I lof to chew on chewing gum!
I lof to see der moon shine owit—"

"And love to eat my sauerkraut,"

added Tom gaily. "Songbird, can't you get up some real nice bit of verse about sauerkraut and Limburger cheese for Hans' benefit?"

"The idea of poetry about sauerkraut and Limburger cheese!" snorted the verse maker in disgust.

"Well, anyway, the lines about the cheese would be good and strong," was Dick's comment.

"A poem about sauerkraut wouldn't do for this automobile age," said Sam, dryly.

"Why not?" asked Tom.

"Because sauerkraut belongs to the cabbage," answered the youngest Rover, and then dodged a blow Tom playfully aimed at him.

"I shan't try to make up any more verses," said Songbird. "Every time I try—"

"Hullo, here comes a carriage with three young ladies in it," called out Dick.

"They look familiar to me," announced Tom. "Yes, they are Dora Stanhope and Grace and Nellie Laning!" he cried.

"Well, this is a pleasure," said Songbird, and forgot all about what he was going to say concerning his verse making.

The carriage was soon up to them. It was a two-seated affair, and on the front seat were Dora and Nellie and in the rear Grace and Mrs. Stanhope.

"We were going to stop at Putnam Hall for a few minutes," said Dora, after the greetings were over. "It was such a lovely day we couldn't resist the temptation to go out for a long drive."

"Sorry we won't be at the Hall to receive you," answered Dick, and he gave Dora such an earnest look that the pretty girl blushed.

"The girls have something up their sleeve," said Mrs. Stanhope. "And they wanted to see you and Captain Putnam about it."

"We are getting up a little party," announced Nellie. "It is to come off at Dora's home some time this fall. We wanted to find out if Captain Putnam would let you and a few of your friends come over."

"Oh, he'll have to let us come!" cried Tom. "Why, I wouldn't miss a party for anything!" And he said this so comically that all of the girls laughed.

"We haven't set any date yet," said Grace. "But you'll speak to Captain Putnam about it, won't you? We thought you might make up a party of say eight or ten boys, and come over in the carryall."

"It's as good as done," announced Sam, with a profound bow. "Please put me down on your card for the first two-step."

"Und put me town for a dree-steps," added Hans, and at this there was another laugh.

"I don't know whether we'll have dancing or not," said Mrs. Stanhope. "But we'll try to have a good time."

"Who do you want us to invite—if we can come?" questioned Dick.

"Oh, Dick, we'll leave that to you. Of course we want all who were on the houseboat," and Dora looked at the Rovers and Songbird and Hans.

"With Fred that will make six. Shall I ask Larry Colby and George Granbury?"

"If you want to—and two more. But please don't ask those boys we just met," went on Dora, hastily.

"You mean Tad Sobber and Nick Pell?" questioned Tom, quickly.

"One called the other Nick. He was a very large lad," said Mrs. Stanhope.

"Sobber and Pell sure," murmured Tom. "What did they do?"

"Stood right in the middle of the road and would not get out of the way," explained Grace. "I think they were perfectly horrid!"

"They made us drive around to one side and we nearly went into a ditch," added Dora.

"And then, after we had passed, they burst out laughing at us," continued Nellie. "They certainly weren't a bit nice."

"We'll have to settle with Sobber and Pell for this," said Dick, and his face took on a serious look that bode no good for the cadets who had played so ungallant a part towards his lady friends.

CHAPTER XIV

AT THE ICE-CREAM ESTABLISHMENT

The Lanings and the Stanhopes had been in the best of health since returning from the south. Mrs. Stanhope was no more the pale and delicate person she had been, and her former nervous manner was entirely gone. The cheeks of the three girls were like roses, and it was no wonder that the Rovers thought them the nicest young ladies in the whole world.

"Wish we were in a carriage," observed Tom, after the turn-out had gone on. "Then we might have gone for a drive together."

"I know what Tom would like," said Sam. "A nice buggy and a slow horse, and Nellie beside him—"

"Humph, please change the names to Sam and Grace and you'll hit it closer," answered Tom, his face growing red.

"I'm going to make up a poem about them some day," said Songbird. "I shall call it—let me see—ah, yes—The Three Fair Maidens of Cedarville."

"Don't!" cried Dick. "Songbird, if you dare to do anything like that—"

"You'll have to leave Dora out anyway," said Tom. "If you don't, Dick will get in your wool sure. He—"

"Say, what about Sobber and Pell?" broke in the eldest Rover, his face quite red. "I feel like punishing them for making the ladies drive into the ditch."

"We'll remember it," answered Sam. "If we catch them in Cedarville let's speak of it and see what they have to say for themselves."

"Speaking about a party," observed Songbird, as they approached the village, "do you realize that we haven't had any sort of a feast at the Hall since we got back to the grind?"

"Fred was saying the same thing only a few days ago," answered Tom. "We certainly ought to have some sort of a blow-out."

"Vot you vos going to plow owid?" asked Hans innocently.

"Blow out the stuffings from a mince pie, Hansy."

"Vere you vos plow dem to, Dom?"

"Blow them into your stomach. Have a spread—a feast—a fill-up, so to speak—something to eat, cheese, sandwiches, cake, pie, pudding, jam, oranges, bananas, lard, salt, plum pudding, toothpicks, ice-cream, turnips, and other delicacies," went on the fun-loving Rover, rapidly.

"Ach, yah, I understand now, ain't it! I like dem feasts. Ve haf him in von of der pedrooms alretty yet, hey?"

"If the crowd is willing," said Sam. "For one, I vote in favor

Arthur M. Winfield

of it."

"Second the nomination," put in Tom, promptly. "It is elected by a unanimous vote we have a feast at the school, some night in the near future, at eleven o'clock, G. M."

The idea of a feast pleased all the boys. They always got enough to eat during regular meal hours at the Hall, but there was something enticing in the idea of having a feast on the sly some night in one of the dormitories. They had had a number of such in the past and these had been productive of a good deal of sport.

"Let us go down to the steamboat landing and see if we can see anything of Pell and Sobber," suggested Dick. "If Sobber is going to Ithaca he'll most likely go by the *Golden Star* ."

They were walking along the main street of Cedarville when they chanced to look into the principal candy store. There, in front of the soda fountain, were the bully of the Hall and his crony. They were drinking soda and talking to a young girl who had served them.

"Hullo, here they are!" cried Sam, and came to a halt.

As they looked into the place they saw Tad Sobber reach over the counter and catch the girl clerk by her curls. He held fast, grinning into her face, while she tried to pull away from him.

"The mean wretch!" cried Dick. "He tries to make himself as obnoxious as he can to everybody he meets."

"Oh, please let go!" came in the girl's voice through the open doorway. "You hurt me!"

"Don't worry, I won't hurt you," replied Sobber, still grinning.

"But I—I don't want my curls pulled," pleaded the frightened girl. "Oh, please let go, won't you?"

"I want you—" began the bully, but did not finish, for at that moment he felt Dick's hand on his ear. Then he received a yank that pained him exceedingly.

"Ouch!" he yelled, and dropped his hold of the girl. "Oh, my ear! Dick Rover, what did you do that for?"

"I did it to make you behave yourself," answered Dick, sternly. "Sobber, I didn't really think you could be so mean," he went on.

"I—I wasn't hurting the girl," grumbled the bully. "And it's none of your business anyway," he added, suddenly, in a blaze of passion.

"After this, you leave her alone."

Tad Sobber glared at Dick for an instant. Then he raised his glass of soda and attempted to dash it into Dick's face. But Sam saw the movement, knocked up the bully's arm, and the soda went into Nick Pell's ear.

"Hi, stop!" roared Nick Pell, as the soda trickled down his neck. "What did you do that for?"

"It was Sam Rover's fault," answered Sobber.

"My brand new collar is spoilt!"

"Charge it to your crony," said Tom.

"I'll fix you fellows!" roared the bully, and raised the empty soda glass over Dick's head. But now Tom rushed in and wrenched the glass from Sobber's hand. In the meantime the girl behind the counter had become more frightened than ever and she ran to the back of the store to summon assistance.

It looked as if there might be a regular fight, but in a few seconds the proprietor of the store appeared, armed with a mop stick he had picked up. He happened to be the father of the girl, and she told him how Tad Sobber had caught her by the hair.

"See here," began the candy store keeper, and flourished his mop stick at the bully. Then Sobber retreated from the establishment and Nick Pell did likewise, and both started on a run up the street.

"What do you cadets mean by coming in here and annoying my daughter?" demanded the storekeeper hotly. "If you can't behave yourselves, you had better keep away."

"We didn't hurt your daughter," said Sam.

"My brother here did what he could to save her from annoyance," said Tom.

"Oh, I know you cadets! You are all tarred with the same brush!" muttered the storekeeper. "I want you to get out— and stay out!"

"Yes, but—" began Dick.

"No 'buts' about it, young man. I want you to get out."

"Father, he made the other boy let go of my curls," explained the girl. "He caught the other boy by the ear."

"That may be, Fanny, but these young bloods are all alike. I don't want their trade. They must clear out, and stay away."

"Come on, fellows," said Dick. "We'll not stay if we are not wanted." He turned again to the storekeeper. "But I want you to remember one thing: We had nothing to do with annoying your daughter."

"Did they pay for the soda?" asked the man suddenly.

"No," replied the girl.

"Then this crowd has got to pay," went on the storekeeper, unreasonably. "How much was it?"

"Ten cents."

"We haven't bought anything and we'll not pay for anything," said Sam.

"Not a cent shall I pay," put in Songbird.

"Did vos a outrages!" burst out Hans. "Of you insult us some more I vos call a bolicemans alretty!" And he puffed up his chest indignantly.

"Well, you get out, and be quick about it!" cried the man, and raised his stick. "Don't let me catch any of you in here again either!"

"Don't worry,—we can spend our money elsewhere," said Tom.

"Where we are treated decently," added Dick, and walked

Arthur M. Winfield

from the candy store.

Once outside, the boys talked the situation over for all of ten minutes, but without satisfaction. All were indignant over the way the storekeeper had treated them, and Tom wanted to go back on the sly and play a trick on him, but Dick demurred.

"Let it go, Tom. He is a mean man, that's all."

"Well, I am going to show folks how generous he is," answered Tom, with a sudden grin. "Wait here a few minutes," and he darted into a nearby store where they sold stationery. When he came out he had a good-sized sheet of paper in his hand and also several big red seals.

"What's that?" asked Sam.

"It's a sign for the candy storekeeper's front window."

With caution Tom went back to the store. He saw that the proprietor was in the rear parlor, dishing out ice-cream to several customers who had come in. The girl was also at the back. Swiftly Tom stuck the sheet of paper up under the show window, fastening it with the gummy seals. The paper read as follows:

FREE BOUQUETS OF ROSES TO ALL YOUNG LADIES BUYING ICE-CREAM HERE TO-DAY. COME IN!

"Now let us watch for some fun," said Tom.

They had not long to wait. The steamboat had come in and a number of passengers were walking up the street. Soon a party of three girls and a young man espied the sign.

"Oh, Clara," cried one of the girls. "Free roses this time of year, just think of it!"

"Come on right in," said the young man, and led the way into the store. Then another young man came along with a girl and they also read the sign and entered. Soon two old maids stopped and read the announcement.

"I do love ice-cream, Angelina," said one. "Let us go in and get chocolate and get the bouquets, too." And they followed the crowd inside.

The store had two side windows to it, which were opened a few inches from the bottom for ventilation, and the cadets stole up to these windows to listen to the talk. Everybody ordered cream and began to eat, and then asked for the bouquets.

"Bouquets?" asked the storekeeper, mystified.

"Why, yes," said the young man who had brought in the three girls.

"If you don't mind, I'd like Jack roses," said one of the maidens.

"And I like American Beauties," said another.

"I don't care what kind I get so long as it is a big bunch," added the third girl.

"What are you talking about?" demanded the storekeeper.

"We are talking about the bouquets you are giving away," said the young man. He had eaten nearly all of his cream and the girls had almost finished.

"I am giving away no bouquets."

"Why, yes you are!" cried the girls.

"Of course!" put in one of the old maids, suspiciously. "And I want just as good a bunch of roses as anybody."

"So do I," added the second old maid.

"Are you folks all crazy?" demanded the storekeeper. "I am not giving away anything."

"What!" demanded the young man who had come in with one girl. "Your sign don't read that way. It says 'free bouquets of roses to all young ladies buying ice-cream here to-day.' You've got to give this young lady her bouquet or I won't pay for this cream!"

"Where is that sign?" demanded the storekeeper, and when told rushed out and tore the announcement down and into shreds. "This is a—an outrage! I didn't put the sign up!"

After this there was a wordy war lasting several minutes. Nobody wanted to pay for the cream eaten, and as he could not furnish the bouquets the storekeeper could not collect. In a rage he chased the would-be customers out and then started to look for the person who had played him such a trick. But the cadets of Putnam Hall had withdrawn from that vicinity and they took good care to keep out of sight.

CHAPTER XV

AN ASTONISHING GIFT

The steamboat had to take on considerable freight at Cedarville, so she remained at the little dock for the best part of half an hour. During that time the Rovers and their friends saw Tad Sobber and Nick Pell walking around the village, but did not speak to them.

"Hullo, here is something new," said Songbird, as they walked past the stores. "A dime museum!"

"Such a thing as that will never pay here," was Dick's comment. "Not enough people."

"It is to remain only one week," said Sam, after reading the sign over the door.

"Wonder if they really have one hundred snakes in the collection?" mused Tom, also reading the sign. "If so, there would be some fun if the bunch broke loose."

"Want to go in and look at the snakes?" asked Songbird.

"I ton't," answered Hans. "Of I look at so many of dem nasty dings I couldn't sleep for a month or sefen days, ain't it!"

And he shuddered.

While the boys were walking away they chanced to look back and saw Tad Sobber and Nick Pell come from the "museum," so called. The bully was talking to a man connected with the show, a fellow who usually stood outside, "barking" as it is called,—that is, asking folks to come up and walk in and see the wonders inside.

"Sobber must know that fellow," was Dick's comment, but thought no more of this until long afterwards. A little later they saw the bully embark on the steamboat, and Nick Pell started back for Putnam Hall alone.

The boys purchased the things they wanted and returned to the school. They did not see Nick Pell until the following day, and then the latter paid no attention to them. Sobber did not return to Putnam Hall for the best part of a week. Then he appeared very thoughtful and he eyed all of the Rover boys in a crafty, speculative way.

"He has got it in for us," said Tom, but how much Tad Sobber "had it in" for the Rovers was still to be learned.

The boys had not forgotten about the proposed feast, and it was arranged that it should come off in the dormitory occupied by the Rovers and some others on the following Tuesday night as soon as all the lights were out. Word was passed around quietly, and the Rover boys thought that only their intimate friends knew of what was going on, but they were mistaken.

By pure accident Nick Pell overheard Larry Colby and Fred Garrison speaking of the feast. It had been arranged that Larry and Fred should contribute a big raisin cake and the two boys were wondering how they could get it from the bake shop in Cedarville and up to the dormitory without being seen.

"Never mind, we'll manage it somehow, if we have to use a rope," said Larry.

"They are going to have a spread," said Nick Pell, running up to Tad Sobber with the story. "We ought to tell Captain Putnam and spoil things for them."

"That won't do us any good, Nick," answered the bully. "The captain thinks too much of the Rovers—he wouldn't punish them much, especially as this is their last term here. I'll think up something else. I want to do something to 'em that they will remember as long as they live."

"You seem to be extra bitter against the Rovers since you got back from Ithaca," said Pell, curiously.

"Am I? Well, I have good cause to be bitter," growled Tad Sobber. "Just let me put on my thinking cap, and I'll fix 'em, and don't you forget it!"

That night the bully asked for permission to go to Cedarville on important business. He went alone, and once in the town hurried directly to the museum already mentioned. The proprietor had done little or no business in the village and was about to move to another place.

When Tad Sobber returned to Putnam Hall he carried under his arm a heavy pasteboard box which he carried with great care. This box he hid away in a corner of the barn, among some loose hay.

"I'm ready to fix the Rovers now," he told Nick Pell. "Keep your mouth shut but your eyes wide open."

Arthur M. Winfield

"What are you going to do?"

"Just wait and see."

At the appointed time the Rovers and their chums assembled in the dormitory for the feast. A large quantity of good things had been procured, including chicken sandwiches, cake, oranges and lemonade. Tom had even had a dealer in Cedarville pack him up several bricks of ice-cream, and these now rested in some cracked ice in a washbowl.

"Say, but this is a touch of old times," said Sam. "Do you remember the first feast we had here, when Mumps got scared to death?"

"Indeed I do!" cried one of the other students. "Here's to the good old times!" and he raised his glass of lemonade to his lips.

In a short while the feast was in full swing. There was a hall monitor supposed to be on guard, but Tom had bought him off with a slice of cake, some candy and an orange, and he was keeping himself in a front hallway, where he could not hear what was going on.

"If it wasn't for the noise, we might have a song," said Sam. "As it is, I move Songbird recite 'Mary Had a Little Cow,' or something equally elevating."

"I can give you an original bit of verse which I have entitled, 'When the Blossoms Fill the Orchard, Molly Dear,'" answered the doggerel maker.

"Gracious, that sounds like a new nine-cent piece of sheet music," murmured Dick.

"Can't you whistle it?" suggested Tom. "It may sound better."

"Play it out on a fine-tooth comb," suggested Larry.

"Who is ready for ice-cream?" asked Tom, after a general laugh had ensued. "This isn't going to keep hard forever."

All were ready, and the bricks were cut, the pieces laid on tiny wooden plates which had been provided, and passed around. Then came more cake and fruit.

In the midst of the jollification there came a sudden and unexpected knock on the door.

"Who can that be?" whispered several in alarm.

"Put out the lights!" said Tom. "Those who don't belong here get under the beds." And he began to get the evidences of the feast out of sight, Dick and Sam assisting him.

With quaking hearts the merry-makers waited for the knock to be repeated, and waited to hear the sound of Captain Putnam's voice or that of the first assistant teacher.

"Bartlett might have warned us," whispered Fred. Bartlett was the monitor who had been bribed.

No other knock came on the door, nor did anybody demand admittance. The boys waited for several seconds, each holding his breath in anxiety.

"Who can it be?" asked Sam of his oldest brother.

"I suppose I might as well go and see," said Dick. "Maybe some of the other fellows are up to some tricks."

With caution he approached the hall door and opened it. Only a dim light was burning, and for the instant he could see nothing. Then he caught sight of a white object on the floor and picked it up. It was a pasteboard box, tied with a strong string.

"This must be some kind of a joke," he said, and came back into the dormitory with the box in his hands. "Light up and let me see what this is."

The lights were lit and several of the boys began to eat the stuff that had been swept out of sight. They all gazed curiously at the pasteboard box.

"Here's a card on the top," said Dick, and commenced to read it. The inscription was as follows:

To the Rover Boys From Their Friends, Dora, Grace and Nellie.

Keep it a secret among you and your chums at the feast.

"How in the world did they know we were going to have a feast?" questioned Sam.

"And how did they manage to smuggle the box into the Hall?" asked Larry.

"Open it and see what's inside, Dick," came from Tom. "I'll wager they have sent us something good."

"Maybe it's a loaf cake," said Fred.

"Oder a pudding," broke in Hans. "I lof chocolate puddings, yah!"

"You can't pack a pudding in a box very well," commented Songbird.

Holding the box in one hand, Dick undid the string and threw off the cover.

The next instant he let out a yell of horror and Tom, who was near by, did likewise and fell over a chair in his fright.

For out of the box glided a real, live snake, fully three feet long, and with beady and dangerous looking eyes!

Arthur M. Winfield

CHAPTER XVI

THE HUNT FOR A SNAKE

"It's a snake!"

"And it's alive!"

"Look out, or he'll bite you!"

"There he goes on the floor!"

These and a number of other cries rang through the dormitory as the cadets saw the contents of the box. Several tried to back away, and Hans pitched over Tom and both went in a heap.

"Ton't you let dot snake bite me!" roared the German youth.

"Maybe he's poisonous!" came from Larry. He had sought safety by leaping on a bed.

Slowly the snake had lifted itself from the box, to glare at several of the boys. Then its cold, beady eyes were fixed on Dick and it uttered a vicious hiss. This was more than the eldest Rover could stand and he let box and snake drop in a hurry. The snake glided out of sight under a bed.

"This is a joke right enough," murmured Sam. "Wonder who played it?"

"Do you think the girls would send a snake?" queried Larry.

"Of course not," answered Tom, who had scrambled up. "This is the work of some enemy."

"Look out! The snake is getting busy!" screamed Sam, and he was right; the reptile had left the shelter of the bed and was darting across the room, in the direction of Songbird.

The would-be poet did not stop to argue with his snakeship, but letting out a wild yell leaped to the top of a small stand which stood in a corner. The stand was frail and down it went with a crash, the wreckage catching the snake on the tail. It whipped around and made a lunge at Songbird's foot, but the youth was too nimble and leaped on the bed.

"We've got to kill that snake," observed Dick, after the reptile had disappeared for a moment under a washstand. "If we don't—"

Crash! It was a plate which Sam shied at the snake, as its head showed for a moment. Then down went a shower of shoes, brushes, plates, and a cake of soap. But the snake was not seriously hurt. It hissed viciously and darted from one side of the dormitory to the other, and made all the boys climb up on the furniture.

"This racket will wake up everybody in the school," said Dick, and he was right. The boys had hardly time to get the most of the evidence of the feast out of the way when they heard a knock on the door.

"Look out there!" yelled Tom. "Don't open that door if you

value your life!"

"What's the matter?" came in George Strong's voice.

"A snake!" answered Dick, and then went on in a whisper: "Quick, boys, get the rest of the stuff out of the way!"

His chums understood, and the remains of the feast were swept under bed covers in a jiffy.

"Did you say there was a snake in there?" demanded the teacher.

"Yes, sir," said Sam. "He's right close to the door now." And what he said was true.

Thinking the youngest Rover might be fooling, the first assistant teacher opened the door cautiously and peered into the dormitory. Then he, too, let out a cry of alarm, for the snake darted forward and made as if to bite him in the foot. Not to be caught he fell back, leaving the door open about a foot. Through this opening the snake glided and disappeared in the semi-dark hallway.

By this time Putnam Hall was in an uproar, and boys were pouring into the hallways demanding to know if there was a fire or a robbery. Soon Captain Putnam appeared, wrapped in a dressing robe and wearing slippers.

"Beware, all of you!" cried George Strong. "It's a snake and it is loose in this hallway somewhere."

"A snake!" ejaculated the master of Putnam Hall. "Where did it come from?"

"It was in the dormitory over there. I heard a noise and went to see what was the matter and the snake came out of the room and made off in that direction," and George Strong pointed with his hand.

"Humph!" muttered Captain Putnam. "This must be looked into. What kind of a snake was it?"

"I don't know, sir, but it was fully three feet long, and it hissed loudly as it went past me."

"Some more of the boys' tricks, I suppose. But this is going too far, especially if the reptile is poisonous."

Lights were lit and turned up as high as possible, and a search of all the hallways followed. When the cadets learned that a snake was really at large in the school many of the timid ones were badly frightened.

"He might poison a fellow and kill him," said one lad.

"Oh, I can't bear snakes," said another. "If he came for me I'd have a fit sure."

The search for the snake was kept up the best part of an hour, but without success. Peleg Snuggers was forced to join in the hunt and nearly collapsed when he saw something under a stand in a far corner.

"The snake! The snake!" he yelled and started to run away. But what he had seen proved to be nothing but a piece of old window cord, and the general utility man was laughed at so heartily he was glad to sneak out of sight.

"He must have gone downstairs," said Dick, and then a hunt was made below. Here some windows had been left open for ventilation, and Captain Putnam said it was possible the reptile had made its escape in that manner. He did not quite believe this, but he thought the snake must be harmless, and he wanted to say something to quiet those pupils who were timid.

"How did the snake get in your room?" he asked later on of the Rovers and their dormitory fellows.

"It came in this box," answered Dick, and brought forth the pasteboard box in question. "Somebody knocked on the door and when we opened it the box was on the floor."

Captain Putnam looked at the box and the inscription.

"Your lady friends must have peculiar tastes," he said, smiling.

"Of course that was a trick—just to get us to take the box and open it," answered Tom.

"Do you suspect anybody, Thomas?"

"Well—not exactly," said the fun-loving Rover, slowly.

"What have you to say, Samuel?"

"I'm sure I can't imagine who could send that box."

"Richard, what can you tell of this?"

Dick paused and took a long breath.

"I can't tell you anything, just now, Captain Putnam," he answered slowly. "But I've got something of an idea of how that box got here. But I'd hate to accuse anybody unless I was sure of it."

"Mr. Strong said the snake was at least three feet long."

"It was certainly all of that."

"Was it a poisonous snake, do you think?"

"It was not a rattlesnake, nor was it any kind of a snake such as are usually found in this part of our country, of that I am sure."

"You got a good look at it then?"

"Yes."

"I certainly had no idea snakes of such size could be found close to the school."

"I am pretty sure that snake was never found around here. During my travels I have studied snakes a little, and that variety was a stranger to me."

"I see." The master of Putnam Hall mused for a moment. "Well, it is very queer. But, as the snake has disappeared, I think we may as well retire once more. I do not imagine we have anything to fear."

It was a good hour before the school was quiet. Many of the boys were afraid to go to bed, and the teachers could not blame them. The Rovers and their chums got together to discuss the situation in whispers and at the same time remove all traces of the feast which had been so curiously interrupted.

"Dick, what do you make of this?" asked Tom.

"I think Tad Sobber is guilty, Tom—but I didn't want to tell

Captain Putnam so."

"You think he got the snake out of that museum?"

"I do."

"I think that myself," put in Sam. "Don't you remember how he was talking to that barker, just as if they were friends? It was surely Sobber who played that trick."

"If it was Sobber we ought to pay him back," came from Songbird, grimly. "A snake! Ugh, it makes me creep to think of it."

"Don't you want to compose an ode in its honor?" questioned Tom, dryly. "Might go like this:

"A hissing, gliding snake
Kept all the school awake;
Each boy in awful fright
Was looking for a bite!"

"You can make fun if you want to, but I think it is no laughing matter," observed Fred. "Supposing a fellow goes to sleep and wakes up to find that snake crawling over him! Phew! talk about nightmares!"

"It certainly would make a fellow feel queer," answered Sam. "But I say, Dick, if you are sure Sobber did it, why can't we pay him back in his own coin?"

"I'm willing, but how can it be done?"

"Wait until to-morrow night and I'll show you," answered the youngest Rover. "That is, unless the snake is caught in the meantime."

"Have you a plan to get square?" asked Larry.

"Yes."

"Den go ahead sure," came from Hans. "Of dot Sobber fellow peen guilty he ought to be hung up on der pottom of der sea alretty quick!"

"Just wait, and we'll fix Mr. Tad Sobber," answered Dick. "He'll wish he never saw a snake." He had an inkling of what was in his brother Sam's mind to do.

CHAPTER XVII

A STIRRING SCENE IN THE SCHOOLROOM

The hunt for the snake was continued all of the next day, but without success. By that time the excitement had died down and a good many of the cadets forgot all about the incident. A few said it must be a joke and they laughed behind George Strong's back.

"It's one of Tom Rover's tricks," said one pupil. "I'll wager he is laughing in his sleeves at Mr. Strong and Captain Putnam."

"Do you think it was a live snake?" asked another.

"No, it was probably a toy affair on a string."

In the secrecy of their room Tad Sobber and Nick Pell laughed heartily over the excitement created—that is, Pell laughed and the bully laughed with him. But Sobber, behind it all, was worried.

The truth of the matter was, he had hoped that the snake would be killed. The man who had sold him the reptile had said it was from Central America and poisonous, but had added that the snake was sick and not liable to do any harm.

Sobber would not have cared had Dick or his brothers been bitten by the snake, but that the reptile was at large was another story.

"Do you think he'd be poisonous enough to kill anybody?" asked Pell, suddenly, and he sobered down as he spoke.

"Oh, no, of course not," answered the bully, but he turned his face away as he spoke. He had given five dollars for the snake and now he was willing to give a like sum to make certain of its death.

In the afternoon Sam led the way to a little case of reptiles which hung on the wall of the school laboratory. In this was a stuffed snake almost the size of that which had disappeared.

"I guess we can frighten Sobber and Pell with that," he said to his brothers.

"Anyway, we can try," answered Tom, falling in with the plan at once.

"We want to be careful of what we do," added Dick. "Otherwise, the pair will smell a mouse."

They talked the matter over, and managed to get the snake upstairs without anybody seeing them. Then they paid a visit to the dormitory occupied by the bully and his cronies and passed some strong black threads across the floor and elsewhere. After that they told Songbird and their other chums of what had been done.

That night Sobber, Pell and their friends went to bed as usual. But hardly had they turned out the lights when they heard a curious rustling sound on the floor near the door.

Arthur M. Winfield

"What is that?" asked Pell, who was inclined to be nervous.

"I don't know, I'm sure," answered Sobber.

The rustling continued, and something seemed to move across the floor. Wondering what it could be, the bully got up and lit a light. Then he gave a yell and leaped back.

"The snake!"

"Where is it?" screamed Pell, sitting bolt upright and his hair raising on ends.

"There it is, over in the corner."

"The snake! The snake!" called out the other boys in the room, and some were so scared that they dove under the bed clothing.

The light was not strong enough to see clearly, and nobody had the courage to make more of an illumination. Sobber stood in the center of the room and as he did this the snake suddenly seemed to fly through the air right at him.

"Oh!" he screamed. "Go away!" and he flopped on his bed and threw a blanket over him. He felt the reptile cross the bed and lay there quaking in mortal terror. Then he heard something moving across the floor.

"That snake is bound to bite me!" he muttered to himself. "Oh, why did I bring it to the school!"

"Call Captain Putnam, somebody!" came from Nick Pell. He was so frightened he could scarcely speak.

There was an emergency bell near the door, to be used in

case of fire, and this one of the boys touched. At once the alarm sounded out, and in a few minutes the hallways were filled with pupils as on the previous night, while some of the teachers and Peleg Snuggers appeared with chemical fire extinguishers in their hands.

"Where is the fire?"

"Shall I telephone for the Cedarville fire department?"

"Has anybody been burnt?"

"What room is it in?"

Such were some of the questions asked. Then Captain Putnam rushed on the scene.

"It's the snake again!" wailed one of the cadets, who now stood bolt upright on his bed, his eyes bulging from his head.

"Are you sure?"

"Yes, the snake is in here," answered Tad Sobber. "Why, it fairly jumped over my bed!"

"He tried to bite me in the face!" came from Nick Pell, who was so excited he scarcely knew what he was saying.

More lights were lit, and Captain Putnam went off to get a shotgun.

"If I catch sight of it, I'll blow it to pieces," he said to George Strong.

A long search followed, and then came a sudden cry from a corner of the dormitory.

"There he is!"

"Shoot him, Captain Putnam!"

The master of the Hall took aim and came up slowly. Then he suddenly dropped the barrel of his shotgun, stepped forward, and took hold of the snake by the tail.

"It's a stuffed snake," he said. "It belongs in the case in the laboratory."

"A stuffed snake?" queried Tad Sobber, and when he realized the truth he was the maddest boy in that school.

"See here," said the master of the Hall, turning to Dick. "Was this what you saw last night?"

"No, sir," was the prompt reply. "What we saw was a real, live snake."

"Indeed it was," said George Strong.

"Are you sure this one is from the case in the laboratory, Captain Putnam?" questioned Andrew Garmore, one of the teachers.

"Yes, I know it well. Besides, here is the label on it."

"Well, I looked at the case early this morning and it was filled as it has always been."

"It's a trick on me!" roared Tad Sobber, angrily. "Just wait, I'll get square with somebody for this!" And he looked sharply at the Rovers.

"Sobber must like snakes—I saw him at the museum in

Cedarville one day," answered Dick, and eyed the bully boldly. At this Sobber grew red in the face and slunk out of sight.

"Get to bed, all of you," said Captain Putnam sharply. "I'll investigate this in the morning."

As on the night before, it took the school a long time to quiet down. The Rover boys and their chums had a hearty laugh over the success of the trick.

"My! but Sobber is mad," said Fred. "You want to watch out, he'll do almost anything to get square."

The promised investigation the next day did not materialize, for the reason that Captain Putnam was called away on important business. Thus two days passed, and the snake incident was again practically forgotten by the majority of the students.

On the following day the master of the Hall came back and said he would start his investigation that afternoon after the school session.

"And let me tell you one thing," he announced. "Whoever brought that real snake into this academy will have to suffer for it."

That afternoon in one of the classrooms some of the pupils were reciting history when of a sudden a wild shriek rang through the air and Nick Pell was seen to bounce up out of his seat and run away from his desk as if a demon was after him.

"What is it, Pell?" demanded the teacher.

Arthur M. Winfield

"The—the snake!" groaned Nick. "Oh, I'm a dead boy!"

"Where is it?" asked a score of voices.

"In my desk! It just bit me in the hand! Oh, I'm a dead boy, I know I am!" And Nick Pell shook from head to foot in his terror.

The announcement that the snake was in Nick's desk was received in various ways by the boys present. Some thought it must be the real snake and others thought it might be only a trick. With caution the teacher approached the desk, armed with a ruler. Then came a hissing sound and the snake stuck out its head.

"It's alive!" yelled a dozen cadets.

"Kill it! Kill it!"

"You go and kill it!"

"I haven't anything."

"Neither have I."

"Throw a book at it," suggested Tom, and let fly his Caesar. His aim was good and the snake was hit in the neck and tumbled to the floor. Then the boys threw books, rulers and inkwells at the reptile, and it was driven into a corner. Dick took up a big geography, let it fall on top of the snake, and stood on it. The reptile squirmed, but could not get away, and in a few seconds more it was killed.

"That's the end of that snake," said Sam, breathing a sigh of relief. "And I am mighty glad of it."

"I am poisoned! I am poisoned!" screamed Nick Pell. "See, my hand is swelling up already!"

"Do you think he was really bitten?" whispered Tom.

"It looks like it," answered Dick. "Too bad—if the snake really was poisonous."

By this time Captain Putnam had come in. He glanced at the dead snake and gave a start.

"Did that thing bite you, Pell?" he questioned.

"Yes, sir, right here—in—the—the palm of the hand," cried the youth addressed. "See how it is swelling."

"I'll telephone for a doctor at once. Come to my office and I will see what I can do for you."

Nick had certainly been bitten and now the hand was twice its ordinary size, while the pain was acute. The boy shook like a leaf.

"I'm poisoned, I know I am!" he wailed. "It's all Tad Sobber's fault, too! Oh, if I should die!" And then of a sudden he fell to the floor in convulsions.

Arthur M. Winfield

CHAPTER XVIII

IN WHICH TAD SOBBER DISAPPEARS

All standing near Nick Pell were amazed to see the boy fall to the floor. Captain Putnam and Dick Rover raised him up. His eyes were rolling frightfully and his jaws opened and shut with a snap that was sickening.

"Something is certainly wrong with him," whispered Sam to Tom.

"Yes, he wouldn't act that way if he was simply frightened," was the reply. "And see his hand!"

"We will carry him up to one of the spare bedrooms," said Captain Putnam. "And, Mr. Strong, see to it that we get a doctor here as soon as possible. Tell him it is a case of snake poisoning, and ask him over the telephone what we had best do."

Nick Pell was carried upstairs. By this time he had ceased to move and lay like a log in the hands of those who supported him.

Many had heard him mention Tad Sobber and all looked at the bully inquiringly. Sobber was deadly pale, but managed to keep up a bold front.

"I am not to blame," he said, in answer to a question from one of the teachers. "I didn't put the snake in Pell's desk."

"Did you bring the snake into the school?"

"Certainly not," answered the bully shamelessly. He made up his mind to keep out of "hot water" even if it was necessary to lie to do it.

A hurry call was sent to Doctor Fremley of Cedarville and he came as quickly as his mare could bring him. Only the teachers and the physician were allowed in the bedroom with Pell, so the cadets did not know what took place.

"It's as plain as day," said Dick to his brother and his chums. "Sobber got the snake and put it in the box. That is why Pell said he was to blame."

"But Sobber told a teacher he did not bring the snake into the Hall," answered Songbird.

"I do not believe him," came from Tom.

"Nor do I," added Sam. "He's a bad egg, if ever there was one."

The poisoning of Nick Pell cast a damper over the whole school, and neither the teachers nor the pupils could settle down to lessons. The doctor remained with the sufferer for two hours, and when he went away he looked very grave.

"He is by no means out of danger," announced the physician. "But let us hope for the best. I think his parents ought to be notified."

This was done, and Mr. and Mrs. Pell came on the very next day to see their son. They found him in something of a fever and out of his mind, crying continually for Sobber to take the snake away.

"Richard, I want to see you," said Captain Putnam that evening, and led Dick to his private office. There he demanded to know what the eldest Rover knew of the snake incident.

"Captain Putnam, I will tell you everything from beginning to end," answered Dick. "If I am to suffer I'll take my punishment, and Tom and Sam say they stand ready to do the same." And thereupon Dick related the particulars of the trouble with the bully and Pell, and of how he and his brothers and Songbird and Hans had seen Sobber and Pell at the museum where the snakes had been. Then he told of the feast, and how the snake had been discovered in the box.

"I have kept the box," he added, "and you can look at the writing if you wish. I think it is in Tad Sobber's hand, although somewhat disguised."

The address on the box was investigated by the master of the Hall, who sent for several compositions Tad Sobber had written. The bully was much disturbed when he had to give up the compositions to George Strong.

"What's that for?" he asked, with a scowl on his face.

"Captain Putnam wants them," answered the teacher, and would say no more.

With anxious eyes the bully watched the first assistant dis-appear into the office with the compositions. Then, looking to make sure that he was not observed, he stole up to the door and applied his ear to the keyhole. What he heard filled him with increased alarm.

"It is Sobber's handwriting beyond a doubt," said Captain Putnam, after comparing the compositions with the address on the box cover. "I wonder if he knew that the snake was a poisonous one?"

"Perhaps Nick Pell can tell that—after he gets over his trouble," returned Dick.

"Provided he does get over it, Richard."

"Don't you think he'll recover?" cried Dick, in consternation.

"He may not. It is a very serious case, so Doctor Fremley informs me."

"What does Mr. Pell say about it?"

"He wants me to investigate. He says he may have somebody arrested for this—and I can hardly blame him. It was a vile thing to do—bring a poisonous snake into the school."

At the mention of arrest Tad Sobber shut his teeth hard.

"I guess it's about time I made myself scarce," he muttered. "Perhaps I had better leave and join Uncle Sid." And he walked away silently and up to his room. He remained there about ten minutes, then stole forth and down a back way, a fair-sized bundle under his arm.

At the conclusion of the interview in the office Captain Putnam sent for Tad Sobber. One of the monitors went on the errand and came back in quarter of an hour with the information that the youth could not be found.

"Did he have permission to leave the grounds?" asked the captain of the teachers.

"Not from me," said one instructor after another.

Then Peleg Snuggers was sent out to hunt the bully up and soon came back with the information that Sobber was not around the grounds, but had been seen by two of the cadets walking in the direction of Cedarville. Sobber had given one of the cadets a note for the master of the Hall. This ran as follows:

"Must go to the village on a matter of great importance. Will explain when I return.—T. Sobber."

"Maybe he has gone to find out about that snake," suggested Tom.

"How could he?" came from his younger brother. "The museum keeper has moved away."

"Tad may know where he moved to," put in Larry.

A whole day passed and the bully did not show himself. Then Captain Putnam drove over to the village and attempted to hunt him up, but without success. He learned that the museum man had shipped his outfit to Boston.

"He has run away," said the master of the Hall to Mr. Pell and George Strong. "I am satisfied now that he was guilty. But as Nick knew of it, he must have had something to do with it," he added.

"I trust my son recovers," answered Mr. Pell, with a deep sigh. But the days went by and Nick Pell still remained in bad shape, very weak and out of his mind for the greater part of the time. During his lucid intervals he told how Sobber had purchased the snake for five dollars, the owner saying it was sick and liable to die in the near future. He added that the bully had said he hoped the snake would bite one of the Rovers.

"I didn't want him to use the snake," said the sufferer, "but he insisted, and told me to keep my mouth shut about it." After that poor Nick began to rave again and had to be given some medicine to keep him quiet. During one of his good spells he was removed to a house located about half a mile from Putnam Hall, where he could get the benefit of absolute quietness. His father went back to business, but his mother remained behind to nurse her boy.

The Thanksgiving holidays were now at hand, but the Rover boys decided to remain at the Hall and not go home until Christmas. Besides, they were preparing for the party at the Stanhope cottage, which was to come off on the following Wednesday evening. They had seen Dora, Nellie and Grace several times, and all had prepared for "the best time ever," as the girls put it. Captain Putnam gave the boys permission to take the carryall and allowed them to leave the school on the day of the party at six o'clock.

"Whoop! here we go!" cried Tom, as he took the whip and cracked it loudly. "Hold on, everybody! Peleg, don't let the team lag," he went on, to the driver.

"An' don't you go for to make 'em run away, Master Tom," answered the driver, grimly.

"It's a pretty long drive and we don't want to be late," said Dick. "So push ahead as fast as you can."

"Say, Tubby, where's your stovepipe hat?" asked Sam of the

Arthur M. Winfield

dude cadet, who formed one of the party.

"I—ah—thought it would not be—ah—quite appropriate," lisped William Philander. "Not—ah—being full dress, you know."

"He was afraid of having it mashed," said Fred. "Hurrah! We're off! Now for a good night's fun!"

They were to have a good night's fun—and a most unusual adventure with it.

CHAPTER XIX

WHAT HAPPENED AT THE PARTY

It was a clear, bright evening when the boys drove over to the Stanhope cottage. All were in high spirits and sang and joked to their hearts' content. For the time being the trouble with Tad Sobber was totally forgotten. So far nothing more had been heard of the bully, and all were satisfied that he had left both Putnam Hall and Cedarville and perhaps for good.

"One boy told me he used to live with an uncle in New York City," said Larry. "He didn't know the uncle's name."

When the carryall arrived at the Stanhope place they found the cottage well lit up. Dora had invited a number of her girl friends and these, with her cousins, Grace and Nellie, were already on hand. The boys let out a ringing cheer as they stopped at the horse-block, and the girls came out to greet them.

"All here?" cried Dora.

"All here," was the answer.

"Good!" cried several of the girls.

Arthur M. Winfield

"I guess we are a bit early," observed Dick. "But we wanted to make sure we wouldn't be late, and it's a long drive over."

"You are not a bit too early," answered Dora, and gave him her dainty hand which he squeezed ardently.

Soon the boys were piling out on the ground, and a general handshaking followed. Those who did not know each other were introduced, and everybody walked into the house, where a room upstairs had been prepared for the cadets' reception.

"Now, everyone must feel perfectly at home," said Mrs. Stanhope, who was being assisted by Mrs. Laning and Mr. Laning. The older folks prepared the refreshments while the young people sat down in the parlor and the sitting room.

At first, as at all parties, there was a little stiffness, but this was soon broken by Tom asking in a solemn voice:

"Say, did anybody bring an iceberg in his pocket? If he did he will please set it on the kitchen stove to thaw out."

"Oh, Tom!" shrieked Nellie, and all the girls giggled. Then the "ice was broken" and everybody started to talk at once. Even William Philander was pleased, for he had discovered a tall, willowy girl who exactly suited him and who thought him charming.

At first they played half a dozen different games and gave out riddles, and Songbird recited a poem written in honor of the occasion. The poem was the best effort he had yet made in the verse line and of course everybody applauded. Then Grace said he ought to have it published in the Cedarville weekly paper, and this pleased the poet very much.

"Maybe you can get a dollar a line for it, Songbird," suggested Dick.

"If he can we'll let him divide up with us," added Tom, and this caused a laugh.

Presently refreshments were announced, and the boys and girls paired off and entered the dining room. Here a long table was spread, decorated with autumn leaves and the Putnam Hall colors. There were six colored candles on the table, each with an elaborate red shade, and the general effect was warm and pleasing. There were plenty of good things to eat, including ice-cream frozen into all sorts of forms. When the forms were passed around, Dick got a drum major, Tom an Uncle Sam, and Sam an airship. Hans got a fat Dutch boy, which tickled him immensely.

"Dot vos look chust like some poys by der Fadderlandt," he observed.

With the ice-cream came snapper bonbons, filled with all sorts of things made of paper, and soon one boy was wearing an apron, another a nightcap, and the like. Dora got a yellow jacket, and Nellie a baker's cap, while Grace skipped around wearing a poke hat over a foot high. There was plenty of laughter, and the old folks did not hesitate to join in. Nuts and raisins followed the ice-cream, and then the young folks went back to the sitting room and the parlor to finish their games and have some music.

"Dora, you must play for us," said Dick, and led her to the piano. Then, while some of the others gathered around, the girl played "Waiting for the Wagon," "Aunt Dinah's Quilting Party," and a number of other favorites, and these the crowd sang lustily.

"Guess it is about time for us to leave," whispered Fred to Dick, presently. "I know you'll like to have Dora play all night for you, but it can't be done."

Dick looked at his watch.

"Phew! as late as this!" he exclaimed softly. "Yes, we'll have to go."

"Let us sing 'Home, Sweet Home,'" suggested one of the boys, and Dora struck up the opening chords. They were in the midst of the first verse when Dick chanced to glance towards one of the windows and stopped short.

A man was outside peering in at the party.

It was Merrick!

"Well, I never!" burst out the eldest Rover boy, and his sudden exclamation caused Dora to look at him curiously and stop playing.

"What is the matter, Dick?"

"Did you see that man at the window? He is gone now."

"I didn't see anybody."

"Who was it?" asked Tom, quickly.

"It was that rascal Merrick!"

"Merrick!" ejaculated Sam. "The fellow who took Uncle Randolph's bonds?"

"The same."

"Oh, Dick, you must be mistaken."

"I was not mistaken—I saw him as plain as day. I am going to look for him," added the eldest Rover, for the man had now disappeared.

He ran for the hall door, and the other boys followed. The girls remained in the parlor, much frightened, for it was after midnight.

As Dick reached the piazza he saw a dark form stealing along a row of bushes near the garden fence.

"There he is!" he exclaimed. "Stop!" he called out, loudly. "Stop, I tell you!"

"Who did you say it was?" asked John Laning, as he came from the kitchen with a stout cane in his hand.

"That rascal Merrick, one of the two men who stole my uncle's traction company bonds," explained Dick.

"What can he be doing here?"

"I don't know. There he goes, over the fence!"

"He is running towards the side road!" exclaimed Sam. "Come on after him!"

"Wait till we get our hats and coats," said Tom, and ran back to pick up the articles mentioned. This took a couple of minutes, and by the time he came back Merrick was out of sight.

The three Rovers ran to the side road, Fred Garrison and Mr. Laning with them.

"I wish I had a pistol," remarked John Laning. "No telling how desperate a character that villain may be."

"I'd like to know if he came on foot or with a horse," said Dick.

"Do you think he followed us to this place?" asked Sam.

"I am sure I don't know. The whole thing looks mighty queer to me."

There was no moon, but the stars were shining brightly, so they could see fairly well on the road. As they reached a bend Tom pointed forward.

"There he is, just going into the bushes!"

"He had better not go that way," was Mr. Laning's remark, "unless he knows the ground well."

"Why not?" asked Sam.

"Just beyond that patch of timber is Nixon's Swamp, as it is called—as boggy and treacherous a spot as can be found for miles around. If he don't look out he'll get stuck there and never get out."

"Do you know the swamp?" asked Dick. "I mean the good spots?"

"Fairly well—I used to come over here when I was a boy— to pick huckleberries. They are plentiful on the other side of the swamp."

"Then supposing you lead the way and we'll follow."

They were soon in the woods and saw a well-defined path running to the eastward. Beyond was Nixon's Swamp, and still further on another woods.

They were afraid they had lost track of the man they were after when they heard a crack ahead of them, followed by a short yell of alarm. Merrick had stumbled over a fallen log and pitched headlong into some thorny bushes. It took him some time to extricate himself, and meanwhile the pursuers drew closer.

"I see him!" cried Tom. "He is turning to the right!"

"He is headed for the worst part of the swamp," was Mr. Laning's comment. "If he doesn't look out—"

A minute later a wild cry rang out from ahead. The cry was repeated twice, and then all became as silent as the grave.

"He must have gone down into the swamp," exclaimed Dick.

"Yes, and more than likely he is drowning to death," added John Laning.

CHAPTER XX

DICK AND DORA

The boys were almost afraid to penetrate further into the woods, for they found the ground growing wet and spongy under their feet. All halted and gathered around Mr. Laning.

"Do you think he has really been drowned?" asked Sam, with a slight shiver.

"It may be," was the farmer's reply. "I know of one man who was drowned here some years ago, and every year cattle are lost here. The bottom of the swamp is very sticky, and once a person gets in he sinks down and under."

"What shall we do?" questioned Tom.

"We can go ahead, but we want to be mighty careful. Don't take a step until you are sure of your footing. If you find yourself sinking, grab hold of some tree or bush."

Mr. Laning led the way and the boys followed, until they had covered a distance of fifty or sixty feet. Here the ground was so soft they had to leap from one tree root or clump of bushes to another. As they moved forward they listened intently for some further sound from Merrick, but none came.

"Hullo, what's this?" cried Dick, presently, and moved to one side, close to a pool of dark and treacherous-looking water. "A man's hat!"

He picked it up and turned it over. On the inside were the initials, S. A. M.

"It must be Merrick's," he went on. "Can he have gone down here?"

The others came at his call and all looked at the hat, which had been lying in the mud at the side of the pool. Then a match was struck, and all gazed around and into the pool while this faint illumination lasted. No other trace of the missing man was to be seen.

"Merrick, where are you?" called out Dick. "If you need help, say so, and we'll try to get you out."

"Do you think he'd answer that call?" asked Fred.

"I think he'd rather go to prison than die in this swamp," was the reply.

The students and Mr. Laning moved cautiously around the edge of the swamp for half an hour and then returned to the roadway. To mark the spot where the hat had been found Dick hung the head covering on a tree limb.

"We can come back in the daylight and make another search," said he. "And we can notify the authorities, too."

When they got back to the Stanhope cottage they found the others anxiously awaiting their return.

"Did you catch him?"

"Did he hurt you?"

"No, we didn't catch him, and nobody is hurt," answered Mr. Laning. "We lost him in the swamp, and there is no telling where he is now."

"I want to get hold of him for two reasons—that is, if he is alive," said Dick. "I want to get back those bonds and I want to know what brought him to this cottage."

"Maybe he came here to rob the Stanhopes," whispered Tom. "But I shouldn't tell them, for it will frighten them too much."

"No, don't say a word, Tom. If you do, Mrs. Stanhope will be just as nervous as she ever was."

"I and my family are going to stay here to-night," announced Mr. Laning; "so we can go on a hunt for that man first thing in the morning."

"And I'll drive over, if Captain Putnam will let me," answered Dick.

The appearance of Merrick had put a damper on the breaking up of the party, and the Rovers were rather silent as they went back to the school. It was too late to speak to Captain Putnam that night, but Dick was up early and saw the master of the Hall before breakfast.

"I trust you had a good time last night," said Captain Putnam, smiling.

"We did have, sir," said Dick. "But our party broke up in a

way we didn't anticipate," and then he told of what had occurred.

The captain had heard of the missing traction company bonds, and he readily allowed Dick to go back to the cottage, using a horse and buggy for that purpose. Sam and Tom wanted to go, too, but to this Captain Putnam demurred.

"I think one is enough, especially as Mr. Laning is there, too," he said.

With a good horse and a light buggy, it did not take long for the eldest Rover boy to reach the Stanhope cottage. The family had just had breakfast and were surprised to see him so early.

"Didn't you have anything to eat?" questioned Dora. "If you didn't, come right in, and I'll make you an omelet and some coffee."

"No, thank you, Dora," he whispered. "I'll have to wait for that until we're keeping house together. Then—"

"Oh, Dick!" she cried and blushed like a rose.

"I had breakfast while driving over,—an orange and some sandwiches," went on the youth. "Mrs. Green got them ready for me. Is there anything new?"

"No. Uncle John is waiting for you. He is in the woodshed, trying on some old rubber boots. He says one ought to have rubber boots to go into the swamp with."

Dick hurried to the woodshed and there found that Mr. Laning had unearthed two pairs of boots, and he donned one pair while the farmer put on the other. A little later both got

Arthur M. Winfield

in the buggy and drove up the road they had traveled the night previous. Then they tied the horse to a tree, and followed the path leading to the edge of the swamp.

"Hullo, the hat is gone!" exclaimed Dick, as he came close to the black pool.

"Maybe it dropped to the ground," suggested John Laning.

Both looked around, but could see nothing of the missing head covering. Then Dick caught sight of a slip of paper pinned to the tree.

"Here is a message of some kind," he said, and read it. The message ran as follows:

"I reckon I fooled you this trip. I was up in the tree all the time. By the time you get this I shall be miles away. Ta ta until the next time."

"Humph!" muttered Dick. "What do you think of that?" And he passed the message to his companion.

"He certainly fooled us," answered Mr. Laning. "I suppose those yells were only to put us off our guard. It's a pity we didn't carry his hat off for a souvenir of the occasion—as you youngsters put it." And the farmer grinned.

"Perhaps he is still around," suggested Dick. "If he tried to fool us once he might try to fool us again."

"That's so, too. It won't do any harm to take a good look around while we are at it, Dick."

They spent the whole of the morning walking around the swamp and in trying to trace the movements of Merrick, but without success. Nothing concerning the rascal was to be found, and when they felt both tired out and hungry they returned to the Stanhope cottage. Here the girls and the ladies had a hot dinner awaiting them and served them liberally, finishing up with apple pie that Dora had made for Dick's especial benefit.

"It's fine!" he said to her, on the sly.

"Then you like it?" she answered, with a smile.

"Do I? Dora, when we're keeping house you shall make me a pie like this twice a week," he added, earnestly.

"Dick, if you don't stop your joking—"

"Oh, I'm not joking, Dora. Of course, if you're not willing to make me a pie now and then—"

"Oh, it isn't that—I'll make all the pies you want. But—but—" And then Dora blushed so furiously that she had to run from the room. Dick looked after her longingly and heaved a mountainous sigh. He wished that all his academy days were over and that he was engaged in business and settled down in life. He knew just what kind of a home he wanted, and who he wanted in it besides himself—and perhaps Dora knew, too.

"But I can't think of those things yet," he mused, as he finished his dinner. "I've got to go out into the world first, get into business, and prove my worth."

The meal over, it was decided that Dick and Mr. Laning should drive to Cedarville and get into communication with the local authorities and also the authorities at Ithaca. This was done, and the following day another hunt was made for

Merrick. But he could not be found; and there, for the time being, the affair rested.

"I think we'll hear from him again some day," said Dick, and he was right; they did hear from the swindler, and when they least expected it.

CHAPTER XXI

A BOB SLED RACE

"Whoop! hurrah! it's snowing!"

Thus shouted Tom one day, as he burst into the library of the Hall, where Dick, Sam and a number of others were perusing books and the latest magazines.

"Hard?" queried Sam, dropping the magazine he held.

"No, but steady. Peleg Snuggers says it is going to be a heavy fall, and he generally knows."

"And he loves snowstorms so," put in Fred, with a laugh. "Do you remember the time we made a big fort and had a regular battle?"

"Indeed I do!" cried Larry. "It was great! We ought to have something of that sort this winter."

"I was hoping we'd get skating before it snowed," put in Songbird.

"Well, we can't have all the good things at once," answered Dick. "I think a heavy snowstorm is jolly. Somehow, when it snows I always feel like whistling and singing."

"And I feel like making up verses," murmured the poet of the school, and went on:

"Oh, the snow, the beautiful snow,
Coming down when the wind does blow.
Coming down both day and night,
Leaving the earth a wonderful sight!
Oh, the snow, the heavenly snow!—"

"Wetting our feet wherever we go!"

continued Tom, and added:

"Oh, the snow,
When the wind doth blow,
It sets a pace
And hits our face
And we are froze
Down to the toes
And in the slush,
That's just like mush,
We cannot stop,
But go ker-flop!"

"Tom, the first thing you know, you'll be taking Songbird's laurels away from him," observed Larry.

"Perish the thought!" answered the fun-loving Rover, tragically.

"I don't hope you call that poetry," came from Songbird, in deep disgust. "Why, Hans can do better than that; can't you, Dutchy?"

"Sure, I can make up some find boetry," answered Hans. "Chust you listen to dis. I make him ub von night ven I couldn't go to sleep."

> "Der vos a leetle pird,
> He sits ubon a dree,
> Dot leetle pird vos habby
> Like von leetle pird could be
> A hunter mit a gun
> Py dot tree did lay,
> He shoot his awful gun,
> And dot pird—he fly avay!

"Good for Hans!" cried Dick, and there was a general laugh. Then the gathering in the library broke up and all the cadets went outside to see how the snow looked. Before long there was enough on the ground to make snowballs, and then a battle royal all around ensued. So long as they took care not to break any windows, Captain Putnam did not mind this, and from his office the master of the Hall and George Strong watched the sport.

"Makes one feel young again," remarked the captain to his first assistant.

"I'd half like to go out myself," answered George Strong.

"I remember one year we had a great snowball fight at West Point," went on the captain. "It was carried out in regular army fashion and lasted half a day. Our side was victorious, but we had to fight desperately to win. I was struck in the chin and the ear, and three of the cadets were knocked unconscious. But it was good practice, for it showed us something of what a hand-to-hand struggle meant."

The snow came down all that day and night, and by the

following morning covered the ground to the depth of about a foot. It was somewhat moist and first-class for the making of snow men and snowballs.

"Let's make a statue of Captain Putnam," said Fred, and this was done, the statue being nearly ten feet high. It must be confessed it was not a very good likeness, but it looked remarkably fierce with some straws for a moustache, a flat wooden stick for a sword, and an old army cap on the top of the head. When he saw it, Captain Putnam laughed as heartily as anybody. Old as he was getting, he never allowed himself to forget the time when he was a boy.

Some distance from the Hall was a fair-sized hill and this was used by the cadets for coasting. As soon as school was over that day the lads brought out their sleds and bobs, and soon the hill was filled with boys, their merry laughter ringing far and wide. The Rovers had a big bob and this was used by the three and also by several of their friends.

"I'll race you!" shouted Dick, who was in charge of the bob. He addressed another student named Peter Slade. Slade had a big bob and had been boasting that this could beat any other bob on the hill.

"All right," answered Slade. He was a lanky youth, rather lazy, and given to much boasting.

It was soon arranged that each bob should carry six boys, and Fred, Hans and Songbird went with the Rovers. The two bobs lined up side by side, and Larry Colby gave the word to go.

"We're off!" shouted Tom, giving a shove, and leaping on behind.

At first the two bobs kept side by side. The slide was in fine condition, and all the other cadets lined up on either side to watch the outcome of the race.

"Hurrah for the Rovers!"

"Hurrah for Peter Slade!"

"May the best bob win!" cried one student, enthusiastically.

"Here's luck to you, Tom!" shouted George Granbury, and threw a snowball that caught Tom in the neck.

"Thanks!" shouted Tom, shaking his fist. "I'll pay that back with interest when I get the chance."

Half of the course was soon covered and still the bobs kept side by side. But then the Rovers' bob began to drag behind.

"Hurrah, we are going to win!" cried one of the boys on the other bob.

"Said I could beat you!" yelled Peter Slade to Dick.

"The race isn't ended yet," flung back the eldest Rover boy.

On and on went the two bobs, and gradually that belonging to Peter Slade drew a full length ahead. Dick glanced back anxiously.

"Something seems to be catching under the runners," he said, "Look and see if everything is clear."

The boys behind looked, and then of a sudden Songbird let out a cry.

"It is Hans' tippet! Hans, go and put that tippet end around your neck and don't let it drag under the bob!"

The German youth was wearing an old-fashion tippet around his neck, the loose ends flying behind. One end had gotten under the bob runners and was scratching along in the snow.

"Vell I neffer!" cried Hans, and pulled on the tippet so vigorously that the long bob began to switch around sideways.

"Look out there!" sang out Sam. "Don't throw us off!"

"Wait, I'll loosen the tippet," came from Songbird, and guided the muffler free of the bob. Then Hans took up the ends and tied them around his waist.

The drag had caused the Rovers' bob to get two lengths behind the other, and Peter Slade and his companions felt certain of winning.

"You can't touch us, Dick Rover!" called Slade, triumphantly.

"Good-bye!" called another boy. "We'll tell those at the bottom of the hill that you are coming."

"Are we making better time?" questioned Tom, anxiously. "If we are not I'll get off and shove," he added, jokingly.

"You hold tight now!" yelled Dick, and an instant later the bob went down over a ridge of the hill. Free of the drag, it shot forth like an arrow from a bow, and soon began to crawl up to Peter Slade's turnout.

"The Rovers are crawling up!"

"Yes, but it's too late to win!"

"We've got to win!" called out Sam.

And then both bobs took another ridge and rushed on to the end of the course, less than a hundred yards away.

Arthur M. Winfield

CHAPTER XXII

PELEG SNUGGERS' QUEER RIDE

The race had now reached its critical point and all of the cadets on the hill waited for the outcome with keen interest. The bob owned by Peter Slade was still two lengths in advance, and it looked very much as if Peter would be the victor.

But with the passing of the last ridge the Rovers' bob seemed to become endowed with new life. With no drag on the runners, it shot forward with a speed that surprised even Dick. Steadily it gained on the other bob, until, when the end of the course was but fifty yards away, the two were almost side by side.

"Let her out, Pete!" cried one of the boys on Slade's bob, but Peter could do no more.

"It's a tie race!" called several, but hardly had the words been spoken when the Rovers' bob shot ahead, and reached the end of the course a winner by twenty-five feet.

"Hurrah! the Rovers win!"

"I tell you what, you can't get ahead of Dick Rover and

his crowd!"

Peter Slade was much chagrinned to have the victory snatched from him, and began to mutter something about the race not being a fair one.

"I agree with you, it was not fair," answered Sam. "Hans' tippet caught under our runners and held us up a good deal."

"If it hadn't been for that we would have won by three times the distance," added Tom.

"Humph!" muttered Peter Slade. "I guess you jumped off once and pushed."

"I did not," answered Tom, hotly.

"I think you did."

"And I say I didn't," and now Tom doubled up his fists.

"Oh, don't quarrel," put in Larry, who was near. "If Peter isn't satisfied why not race over again?"

"I am willing," answered Dick, promptly.

"I'm tired of riding," said Slade. "I—er—I am not feeling extra well and it shakes me up too much."

"Then let some of the others use the bob."

"No, it needs overhauling, and I am going to have it fixed up," was Slade's answer, and began to move off toward the Hall, dragging his bob after him.

"He's afraid to race," said George. "My! how mad it makes

some fellows to get beaten!"

It may be mentioned here that Peter Slade had been one of Tad Sobber's cronies, and now that Sobber was gone he took it on his shoulders to fill the bully's place in the particular set to which he belonged. He was a quick-tempered youth, and had been in more than one fight since his arrival at Putnam Hall.

The boys who could not ride on the hill amused themselves by making some big snowballs, which they allowed to roll down another hill. One of the snowballs made was fully eight feet in diameter, and it was a great sight to see this go down, getting bigger and bigger as it progressed.

"Hello, I've got an idea!" cried Tom, as he watched the rolling of the big snowballs.

"Something brand new, Tom?" queried Larry.

"I think so. Let us give Peleg Snuggers a roll. It will do him good—shake up his liver, and all that."

"You mean to roll him down this hill?" asked a student named Morley.

"That's it."

"Might hurt him."

"Not if we put a snow overcoat on him first," answered Tom.

"What do you mean?" asked another student.

"Let us roll a big ball the shape of an egg and hollow out the middle. Then by some trick we can get Peleg to crawl inside, and—"

"That's the thing!" cried George Garrison. "Come on. Where is Peleg?"

"Down at the stables."

With eager hands the cadets set to work and rolled up a big ball in the shape of an egg and then dug out the middle with a shovel. In the meantime a message was sent to the general utility man that he was wanted at the top of the hill at once.

"Must want me to mend a sled," he mused, and hurried off, taking with him some tools, nails and cord. He often did favors for the cadets, who gave him "tips" in return.

When Peleg Snuggers arrived at the top of the hill the big snowball was ready for use.

"Here is Peleg!" cried Tom. "He can do the trick for us. Can't you, Peleg?"

"What is that, Tom?" asked the general utility man, innocently.

"We want to fasten this cord in the hole through that big snowball, but we don't want to get it crossed," went on Tom, anxiously. "Will you take the cord, crawl in there and then pass the end out and over the end of this shovel, and then loop it over to the other end?"

"Why—er—I don't understand," stammered Peleg Snuggers.

"I'll explain after you are inside the ball," said Tom. "Here's the cord," and he led the general utility man to the hole and helped him to get down.

Not suspecting a trick, Snuggers crawled into the big snowball. Before he could do anything with the cord given to him the cadets rushed forward and gave the snowball a push toward the edge of the hill.

"Hi! stop that!" roared the general utility man, trying to back out.

"Hold tight—the snowball is getting away from us!" yelled Tom. "Somebody keep it from going down the hill!"

"We can't hold it back!" screamed Larry, grinning at the same time.

"It's bound to go—too bad!" wailed another.

"Say, let me git out!" yelled Peleg Snuggers, but at that moment the snowball began to turn over. "I'll be killed! Oh, dear, I think you did this a-purpose, you rascals!"

"Never!" came back promptly.

"Enjoy the ride while you have the chance, Peleg!"

"You've got a free ticket to the bottom of the hill!"

"Let me out! Stop her!" yelled Snuggers, and they saw his feet at one end of the big snowball and his hands at the other. "I can't stand rollin', nohow!"

"You're not standing," called Sam. "You are just rolling."

Away went the big snowball, down the long hill, and the cadets after it. As it progressed it grew larger and larger. They saw Peleg Snuggers shove out his head from one end, and the head went around and around like a top.

"I guess he'll be rather dizzy when the trip's ended," observed Songbird.

At last the snowball came to a stop in a stretch of meadow land. The students rushed up just in time to see Peleg Snuggers crawl out on his hands and knees. When he arose he staggered around as if intoxicated.

"Say, you young villains!" he gasped, and then had to stop to catch his breath.

"Oh, Peleg, why did you run away with our snowball?" asked Tom, innocently.

"It was a mean thing to do," put in Dick.

"We wanted some fun with that ball," added Sam.

"I—run—off—with the—the snowball?" gasped the general utility man. "I want you to know—"

"Oh, we know all about it," interrupted Tom. "I know what's the matter. You've been drinking, and didn't know what you were doing."

"Perhaps we had better report this to Captain Putnam," said Larry. "Drinking isn't allowed around here, you know."

"I hain't drunk a drop—it's the rollin' as made me dizzy," roared Peleg Snuggers. "Oh, dear, I can't stand straight," and he bumped up against the big snowball and sat down in a heap.

"I'll tell you what I think you ought to do," proceeded Tom, calmly. "I think you ought to roll our snowball back up the hill for us."

"Roll it back?" snorted Snuggers. "Why, four hosses couldn't pull that weight o' snow up the hill! I ain't going to tech the snowball."

"Then at least pay us for the ride you've had," suggested Sam.

"I ain't goin' to do that nuther! It's a trick that's what it is!" growled the general utility man, and arose unsteadily. "I'll be sick for a week after this, I know I will!"

"Never mind," said Dick, soothingly. "Just get Mrs. Green to give you a dose of pink Whirl Around Pills, and you'll be all right again."

"I shan't never come out to this hill again, not fer nobody," grumbled the general utility man, and walked off. Then he turned to gaze at the cadets. "You do anything like that again an' I'll tell Captain Putnam on ye, see if I don't. I ain't going to be no merry-go-'round, or spinnin' top fer nobody!" And then he hurried for the stables and disappeared.

CHAPTER XXIII

HOLIDAYS AT THE FARM

Almost before they knew it, the mid-winter holidays were at hand, and the Rover boys went home to enjoy Christmas and New Year. On their way they stopped at several stores in Ithaca, where they purchased a number of Christmas presents. Some of these they mailed at the post-office. Dick sent a nice book to Dora, and Tom and Sam sent books to Grace and Nellie. The boys also united in the gift of a stick pin to Mrs. Stanhope and another to Mrs. Laning, and sent Mr. Laning a necktie. Captain Putnam was not forgotten, and they likewise remembered George Strong. The rest of their purchases they took home, for distribution there.

A number of the other students had come as far as Ithaca with them, and here the crowd had dinner at one of the hotels,—the same place where Tom had once played his great joke on Josiah Crabtree.

"By the way, who knows anything about Nick Pell?" asked one of the students, while dining.

"He has been removed to his home in the city," answered George Granbury.

"Is he better?" questioned Dick.

"They say he is better some days, but at other times he is worse. The poison somehow affected his mind."

"What a terrible thing to happen," murmured the eldest Rover, and then shuddered to think what might have ensued had the snake bitten him.

"Any news of Tad Sobber?" asked another cadet. He looked at each of the others, but all shook their heads.

"It's queer where he went to," said Songbird. "Wonder if Captain Putnam tried to communicate with his folks?"

"He has only an uncle, and the captain couldn't find him," answered another youth who was present.

As the dinner progressed the boys warmed up, and at the conclusion they sang several songs. Then the Rovers had to rush for their train and they caught it just as it was pulling out of the station.

"Hullo!" cried Sam, as he dropped into a seat, and he pointed out of the car window.

"What's up now?" queried Tom.

"I saw a fellow on the depot platform who looked like Tad Sobber!"

"Are you sure it was Sobber?" demanded Dick.

"No, I am not dead certain—but the fellow looked a good deal like Tad."

"Must have been a mistake," was Tom's comment. "What would he be doing around Ithaca?"

"Well, he's got to stay somewhere, Tom."

"But he wouldn't stay so close to Cedarville—he'd probably go to some big city," put in Dick.

As the train rushed on the Rover boys talked the matter over, but could make nothing out of it.

"I suppose he is in hiding waiting to see if Nick Pell will recover," said Dick. "He knows that if Nick doesn't get over his trouble he'll be liable to prosecution."

At the station at Oak Run the boys found their father awaiting them with the big family sleigh. All piled in, and over the crisp snow they started for Valley Brook farm.

"I need not ask how you are feeling," said Anderson Rover. "Every one of you looks the picture of health."

"I never felt better in my life," declared Dick, and Tom and Sam said the same.

"Has Uncle Randolph heard anything more of his traction company bonds?" asked Tom, as they drove along.

"Not a word more," answered his father. "It is a great loss to him."

"Do you suppose the game was tried on anybody else?" asked Sam.

"We have not heard of it."

Arriving at home, the boys were warmly greeted by their uncle and their aunt and also by the others around the house. Their aunt had a hot supper awaiting them, and while they ate this the whole subject of the missing bonds was thoroughly discussed. The boys learned that a private detective was still on the trail of Merrick and Pike, but so far had reported nothing of importance.

"I believe those rascals,—or at least Merrick—must belong around Lake Cayuga," observed Dick. "Otherwise we shouldn't have seen Merrick in Ithaca and up at the Stanhope place."

"I was very simple to let them get the best of me. The next time I shall be more careful," said Randolph Rover.

The boys learned from Jack Ness that hunting in the woods back of the farm was good, and two days before Christmas they went out with the hired man. They went for rabbits and squirrels, and each took his shotgun along and a substantial lunch, for they expected to be out the greater part of the day.

It was clear, cold weather, the sun glistening brightly on the snow. They journeyed directly for a portion of the woods they knew was a favorite spot for rabbits, and it was not long before they started up several.

"There they go!" cried Dick, and took aim. Bang! bang! went his gun, and the reports of Tom's firearm followed. Three rabbits came down, and a few minutes later Sam brought another one low.

"Four for a starter are not so bad," remarked Tom, as the game was placed in their bags. "Even if we don't get any more we won't have to go home empty-handed."

By noon they had made their way directly through the woods and had eleven rabbits and three squirrels to their credit. Then Tom suggested they build a campfire and rest while eating their lunch and this was done.

"I wish we could bring down a fox or two," said Jack Ness. "They have been bothering the chickens again lately— carried off two only night before last."

"Do you know where they hang out?" asked Dick.

"I think they come from over yonder," and the hired man pointed with his hand to the northward.

"Let us travel in that direction after dinner," suggested Sam. "Even if we don't spot any foxes we may find as many rabbits and squirrels there as anywhere else."

The others were willing, and half of the afternoon was spent by the four hunters in a locality that was new to them. One fox was sighted, and Jack Ness shot the animal in the hind quarters, and then Sam finished him by a shot in the side.

"Well, that makes one fox less anyway," said the hired man.

They kept on, and brought down two rabbits and a wild turkey. By this time they were pretty well tired out, and Tom suggested that they start for home.

"It's a long tramp," he said, "and by the time we get back I guess we'll all be ready to rest."

"As for that, I am ready to rest now," said Sam. "Tramping through the snow is no easy task."

"Especially if a fellow's legs aren't very long," returned Dick,

Arthur M. Winfield

with a grin.

"Well, mine are as long as they ought to be," came from Sam, promptly. "They reach to the ground, and yours don't reach any further," and then there was a general laugh, Jack Ness guffawing loudly.

The hired man said he knew of a short cut to the farm, and they followed him to something of a path through the woods and then out on a trail made years before by charcoal burners. Soon they came in sight of a cabin, from the chimney of which the smoke was curling.

"Who lives here?" asked Dick.

"An old man named Derringham," answered Jack Ness. "He is very old and somewhat out of his head. He makes his living by selling herbs and barks for medicine. Years ago, so they say, he was an herb doctor, but he didn't have a certificate, or something like that, so the authorities drove him out of business. After that he got queer and took to the woods."

"Let us go in and see him," said Tom, whose curiosity was aroused. He walked boldly up to the hut and knocked loudly on the dilapidated door.

"Who is that, Pop?" he heard somebody ask, in a startled voice.

"I don't know, sir," was the answer, in the voice of an old man.

"I don't want to see anybody," went on the first speaker. "Send him away, whoever he is."

"Go away!" cried the old man. "I don't want anybody around here."

By this time all of the party outside were at the door. Tom's face showed that he was laboring under sudden surprise.

"Evidently the old man doesn't want visitors," was Dick's comment.

"There is somebody else in there with him," whispered Tom. "From his voice I should say it was Bill Dangler!"

Arthur M. Winfield

CHAPTER XXIV

A CAPTURE AND A SURPRISE

The others were much astonished by what Tom said, and they could scarcely believe that they had heard aright.

"Bill Dangler!" cried Sam, but Tom put his hand over his brother's mouth to silence him. Then he nodded vigorously.

"What would that freight thief be doing here?" questioned Dick, in a whisper.

"I am sure I don't know. But I am almost certain it was Dangler's voice. If you will remember, it has a certain shrillness to it."

"Yes, I know that."

During this talk there were murmurs in the cabin which those outside could not understand. Then the old man came towards the door and slipped a bolt into place.

"I want you to go away!" he said sharply. "I don't like strangers around here."

"We won't hurt you, Mr. Derringham," said Dick. "We came

to pay you a friendly visit."

"Wouldn't you like a nice rabbit from us?" asked Tom, bound to get into the cabin somehow.

"I have no money with which to buy rabbits."

"We'll make you a present of one," said Sam.

"I want no presents from anybody. I want you to go away," said the old man, in a high-pitched, nervous tone.

"Mr. Derringham, don't you remember me?" asked Jack Ness. "I used to buy herbs and watercress from you. I'd like to speak to you for a minute."

"Who are you?"

"I am Jack Ness, the man who works over on the Rover farm."

"The Rover farm!" muttered a voice in the cabin. "Don't let them in! Don't you do it!"

"I am sure that is Dangler!" cried Tom, whose ears were on the alert. "If he is really there we have him cornered!"

"Yes, and he shan't get away from us again," added Dick.

"If he tries it we can halt him with a dose of buckshot," put in Sam.

After that there was a pause, the boys not knowing exactly how to proceed. Tom pressed on the door, but it refused to give way.

Arthur M. Winfield

"I tell you I want you to leave!" cried the old man, after some more whispering in the cabin. "If you don't go away I'll get my gun."

"There are four of us and all armed," answered Dick. "So you had better not do any shooting. But you have got to open that door. We will do you no harm."

"What do you want in here?"

"We want to see who is in there with you?" answered Tom, boldly.

"Don't you know that I am alone?"

"You are not alone," said Sam.

"Well, I know best," was the hesitating answer. "If I was sure you wouldn't hurt me I'd let you in."

"We will not harm you in the least," answered Dick.

There was a moving around in the cabin and what seemed to be the dropping of a door. Then old Derringham came forward again.

"You are sure you won't rob me if I open the door?" he asked.

"We mean you no harm—if you will do what is right," said Tom.

Then the door was thrown open and the Rover boys and Jack Ness were confronted by a man at least seventy years of age. He had snow-white hair and a snowy beard that reached to his waist.

The boys and the hired man went hastily into the cabin and looked around. Nobody but Derringham was in sight. Dick looked at the floor under the table and saw something which looked like a trap door.

"He must have gone into the cellar," said he to the others, and made a movement forward.

"Stop, do not touch that table!" cried the old man, in alarm.

"Mr. Derringham, listen to me," said the eldest Rover boy firmly. "We are after a criminal—a man who for years robbed the railroad company of valuable freight. We know he is somewhere around your place. If you shield this criminal, or aid him in getting away, you will be guilty of a crime."

At this strong assertion the old man began to tremble, and he looked from one to another of those before him in alarm.

"I—I Bill Dangler said it was not true—that it was a plot against him," he murmured.

"It is true, and there is no plot against him, excepting to make him pay the penalty of his crimes," put in Tom. "If you have hidden him you had better give him up."

"I know you," said old Derringham, turning to Jack Ness. "You used to pay me good prices for what you bought of me. Can I trust you?" he went on, pleadingly.

"Certainly you can, and you can trust these boys, too," was the hired man's reply. "If you want to keep out of trouble you had better help us all you can."

By this time Dick had the table shoved to one side. Under the bottom of one of the legs he found a small iron ring, connecting with the door in the floor. He pulled on this and the door came up, showing a small cellar below, used chiefly by the old man for the storage of winter vegetables and the roots he gathered.

"Dangler, you might as well come up!" called out Dick. "It won't do you any good to try to hide."

"What do you want of me?" came in a sullen voice from below.

"You know very well what we want."

"I haven't done anything."

"You can tell that to the police, after you are locked up. Come up."

Slowly and with downcast face Bill Dangler crawled from the small cellar and pulled himself up to the floor of the cabin. He gazed reproachfully at the old man, who was again trembling.

"I'll fix you for going back on me," he muttered.

"They say you are a thief," answered the old man. "If you are, I want nothing more to do with you. I am poor, but I am honest—everybody who knows me knows that."

"He shall not harm you," put in Tom. "He'll soon be behind the bars."

A glance at the party of four, with their shotguns, convinced the freight thief that escape was out of the question.

"I suppose I'll have to give up," he growled. "But I ain't as guilty as you may think I am."

"You are guilty enough," said Sam.

"I didn't plan those freight robberies."

"Who did then?" questioned Tom.

"Merrick and Pike. I don't mind telling on them, for they have gone back on me."

"Is Merrick the head of the gang?" asked Dick.

"Yes."

"Where is he now?"

"If I tell will you let me go?"

"I can't do that, Dangler."

"Well, I don't care anyway. Merrick hasn't treated me right, and he ought to suffer. He has a hangout a few miles from the city of Ithaca, if you know where that is."

"Yes, on Lake Cayuga."

"That's it."

"You say a few miles from the city," pursued Sam. "What do you mean by that?"

"He and some of his friends, Pike among them, have a meeting place along the lake. It's an old house, unpainted, and with very narrow windows, so I've been told. You find that house and likely you'll find Merrick and Pike."

"I thought those chaps were from the city?" said Sam.

"They are, but every once in a while they find it convenient to disappear, and then they go to that place on Lake Cayuga. It's an old homestead that used to belong to Merrick's sister."

"We ought to be able to find that place," said Tom to his brothers. "Especially if it was a homestead."

"Was the sister's name Merrick, too, or was she married?" asked Sam.

"She was a widow, so I was told. When she died she left her son in charge of Merrick—but I don't believe he ever looked after the boy very much."

"What was her name?" asked Dick.

"Sobber—Mary Ann Sobber."

"Sobber!" ejaculated the three Rover boys.

"That's it."

"Did you ever hear the son's name?" asked Dick.

"I don't remember—yes, I do. Merrick had a letter from him once. The boy's name was Tad Sobber. He was at a boarding school somewhere."

CHAPTER XXV

CHRISTMAS AT THE FARM

"What do you think of that?"

"Isn't that the greatest ever!"

"Well, I'm sorry for Tad."

Such were the exclamations from the three Rover boys after listening to Bill Dangler's declaration that the lad who had run away from Putnam Hall was the nephew of Merrick.

"Are you certain of this?" asked Dick.

"Certainly I am. But why are you so interested in Merrick's sister and her son?"

"I will tell you," answered Tom. "Tad Sobber used to go to school with us, but he ran away a short while ago and we haven't heard from him since."

"Phew! so that's it! Maybe he's with his uncle."

"Like as not. I wonder if he knows his uncle is a thief?"

Arthur M. Winfield

"I don't know anything about that. Sid Merrick is a sly one and can put on the most innocent front you ever saw."

"What do you know about Pike?"

"Oh, John Pike is only a tool, same as I was."

After that Bill Dangler seemed anxious to relieve his mind, and he related many of the particulars of the freight robberies. He said that all had been planned by Sid Merrick, and that two other men were implicated besides himself and Pike and named the men. He said that Merrick had sold the stolen stuff in various large cities.

"Did he divide with the others?" asked Dick.

"He was supposed to do it, but I don't think any of us ever got our full share."

Old Derringham listened to the thief's recital with keen interest. But presently he rushed forward and caught Bill Dangler by the arm.

"I want you to go!" he cried, almost fiercely. "I want no thief under my roof!"

"He shall go, and at once," declared Dick. "It is getting late, and it is a long tramp to Oak Run."

"He owes me a dollar for keeping him several days," went on the old man.

"Then he had better pay you," said Tom.

Dangler wanted to demur, but in the end he paid for his board, and then the whole party left, the old man gazing after them curiously. That he had been entirely innocent in the affair there could not be the slightest doubt.

"Now, Dangler, it won't do you any good to try to get away," said Dick, as they tramped along through the snow. "We are four to one and armed."

"I won't try to run away," was the dogged answer.

"If you give the authorities all the help you can, perhaps, when it comes to a trial, they will be a little easy on you," put in Tom.

"I hope so. I was coaxed into this. I used to be an honest man," responded the freight thief.

"Well, before you die, you'll learn that 'honesty is the best policy,'" observed Sam.

"I've learned that already. I've lost all my old friends, and I can't show myself anywhere any more."

The crowd had to tramp a good mile and a half before they reached a farmhouse where they could procure a team and a sleigh big enough to take all of them to Oak Run. Then they set off at a fast pace and at about supper time reached the Rover farm.

Those at the farm were much astonished at the "game brought in," as Anderson Rover declared. The boys waited long enough to get a meal, and gave the prisoner something to eat, and then they set off for Oak Run with their father and Dangler. Here the freight thief was placed in the custody of the local constable, who locked the man up in the garret of his own home.

Arthur M. Winfield

That night and the next day the telegraph and telephone were kept busy, and some officers of the law from Ithaca visited the old Sobber homestead. They found the place deserted and no trace of Merrick, Pike or Tad Sobber was to be found.

"It is too bad," declared Dick, when the news came in. "I thought sure we'd round up the rascals."

From the authorities the boys learned one thing—that the Sobber homestead was on the same road that ran past the Stanhope cottage.

"That may account for Merrick coming and looking in the window that night," said Dick. "Maybe he was traveling past and wanted to see what was going on."

"More than likely he was looking for a chance to rob the place," was Tom's grim comment.

On Christmas day the boys received a number of valuable presents and gave everybody presents in return. There was a grand family dinner, such as only their aunt Martha could prepare, and it is needless to say that all did full justice to the spread. After dinner the lads went out snowballing and got Aleck Pop and Jack Ness to do the same. The boys snowballed the colored man and Jack Ness so vigorously that the pair had to run for the barn.

"My sakes alibe, boys!" cried Aleck Pop, after he had received a snowball in the ear. "Yo' dun work yo' snowballs lik da was comin' from a Gatling gun!"

During the week between Christmas and New Year, Bill Dangler was removed to the county jail, there to await the action of the grand jury. In the meantime the authorities continued the hunt for Merrick, Pike and the others, but without success.

"I'd really like to know what has become of Tad Sobber," remarked Dick. "It is a pity if he is dependent upon such a fellow as Merrick for his support."

"Perhaps his mother left him money," said Tom.

At last came the day when the boys returned to Putnam Hall. On the train they fell in with Larry Colby and George Granbury, and told of what they had learned.

"I heard from Nick Pell yesterday," said Larry. "He is getting better gradually, but it will be some time before he is himself again."

"Does he still blame Tad Sobber?"

"Yes, and he says he will never have anything to do with Sobber again."

"Nobody can blame him for that," said Sam.

"I don't believe Sobber will ever return to Putnam Hall," came from Tom. "Especially when he finds out that we know he is the nephew of such a swindler as Merrick."

In a few days the boys settled down again to their studies. The Rovers were exceedingly anxious to make records for themselves, and whenever a lesson was too hard for Tom or Sam, Dick helped them all he could. The eldest Rover boy was sorry he had missed his former position by being absent, but he was delighted to know that he and his brothers would now finish their schooling at Putnam Hall together.

"I couldn't bear to think of being separated from you," he

said to Tom and Sam.

"We don't want to be separated," returned Tom.

"That's the talk!" declared Sam. "We'll stick together always!"

About a week after the return to school the snow cleared away and then came a cold snap that made excellent skating. At once all the boys got out their skates, and during their off hours they had great fun on the lake.

One afternoon a race was arranged between half a dozen boys, including Dick, Larry Colby and Peter Slade. Slade was sure he would win, and went around boasting of it.

"I have been in six races on skates," he declared, "and I won every one of them."

"He must be a famous skater," said Tom, when he learned of this. "Dick, I don't think you'll stand much show against him."

"I don't know. Do you know what I think of Peter Slade? I think he is a big blower."

"I think that myself. Still, if he has won six races he must know something about racing."

"Well, if I lose I shan't cry over it," said Dick, and there the talk ended.

The race was to be for two miles,—a mile up the lake shore and a mile back. At the appointed hour the contestants lined up, and at a word from George Strong, who had consented to start them, they were off.

It was easy to see that Peter Slade was a good skater, and with hardly an effort he went to the front during the first quarter of the race. But then Larry and Dick began to push him, and when the mile turn was made Larry was but two yards in the rear, with Dick almost on his heels.

"Go it, Slade, you can win easily!"

"Catch him, Larry!"

"Put on more steam, Dick!" yelled Tom, enthusiastically.

And then the turning point was passed by all the racers and the struggle on the homestretch commenced.

Arthur M. Winfield

CHAPTER XXVI

THE SKATING RACE

For nearly half a mile Peter Slade kept the lead with ease, but then his breath began to fail him. Looking over his shoulder, he saw both Larry and Dick crawling up.

"No, you don't!" he muttered, and put on a fresh burst of speed that increased his lead by two yards.

"Peter Slade is going to win!"

"See how he is running away from the others!"

So the cries arose and it certainly looked as if the youth mentioned could not possibly be defeated.

But now both Larry and Dick "dug in for all they were worth," as they themselves expressed it. While there was yet a quarter of a mile to be covered Dick made a spurt and ranged up alongside of his chum.

"Sorry, but I've got to go ahead!" he cried, gaily.

"Come on, we'll both go!" yelled Larry, good naturedly, and then the pair put on a fresh effort and in a moment ranged up on either side of Peter Slade.

"Hullo, they are in a line!"

"There goes Larry Colby ahead!"

"Dick Rover is going with him!"

"Say, but that is skating, eh? Just look at Dick strike out!"

"Sandwick is coming up, too!"

"And so is Marley!"

The last reports were true. The fourth and fifth boy were now directly behind Slade. As Dick and Larry shot ahead, still side by side, Sandwick overtook Slade and so did Marley. In the meantime the sixth boy had lost a skate and dropped out.

With a final desperate effort Peter Slade tried to gain first place. But his wind was gone and his strength also, and he dropped back further and further.

"Hurrah, here they come!"

"It's a tie race between Dick and Larry!"

"Marley is third!"

"Yes, and Sandwick fourth."

"Peter Slade is fifth."

"Humph! And Peter said he was bound to win!"

Then over the line shot the skaters, Dick and Larry side by

side and laughing merrily. As soon as the race was ended they locked arms to show their good feeling. Then Marley came in with Sandwick at his heels. In deep disgust Peter Slade refused to finish, but circled to one side and hurried to the boathouse, there to take off his skates and disappear.

"It was a well-skated race," declared George Strong. Then he asked Dick and Larry if they wanted to skate off the tie.

"We won't bother," said Dick, after consulting his chum. "We are satisfied to let it stand as it is, considering that there was no prize to be awarded."

The fact that he had lost the skating race made Peter Slade more sour than ever, and after that, whenever he met Dick, he glared at the eldest Rover boy defiantly.

"He acts as if he had a personal grudge against me," said Dick to his brothers.

"Well, he acts that way to me, too," answered Tom.

"He ought to have his head punched well," was Sam's comment.

Peter Slade did not seem to care that Larry had beaten him— his enmity was directed mainly at Dick.

Slade was in one of the lower classes, but one day one of the teachers announced a lecture on the battleships of the American navy, and a large number of boys came in to listen and to take notes.

In the midst of the lecture Dick had occasion to pass down one of the aisles. As he went by Peter Slade the latter put out his hand and hit him in the knee. Slade's hand had ink on it and the ink went on Dick's clean uniform.

"What did you do that for?" demanded Dick, halting.

"Shut up!" whispered Slade, uglily.

"I've a good mind to box your ears," went on Dick.

"Will you?" roared the bully, leaping up. "Just try it!" And so speaking he made a pass at Dick's head.

The blow landed on Dick's shoulder, leaving an ink mark behind it. The eldest Rover boy had leaped to one side. But now he leaped forward, and a well-directed blow from his fist sent Slade reeling backward over a desk.

"Stop that!" cried the teacher, in alarm, and brought his lecture to an abrupt end.

"A fight! A fight!" cried several of the boys, and left their seats to surround Dick and the bully.

Slade was dazed for a moment, but on recovering he sprang at Dick and tried to force him to the floor. Around and around went the pair, bumping against the desks and sending some books to the floor. The teacher tried to get at them, but before he could do so they had separated. Then Dick hit Slade a telling blow in the left eye which caused the bully to fall into a nearby seat.

"Stop, this instant!" cried the teacher, and then turning to some of the boys added: "Summon Captain Putnam at once."

The room was in an uproar, and many wanted Dick and Slade to continue the battle. But the punch in the eye had taken away the bully's courage and he did not get up to

Arthur M. Winfield

continue the contest.

"What does this mean?" demanded Captain Putnam, as he came in, and he faced Dick and Slade sternly.

"It means that that fellow ought to have a good thrashing, sir," answered Dick, boldly, and pointed at the bully.

"It's his fault, it ain't mine," put in Peter Slade, hastily. "He started it."

"That is not true, Captain Putnam. I was passing his seat when he reached out and smeared ink on my knee," and Dick pointed down to his soiled trousers. "I wasn't going to stand for that and told him so. Then he jumped up and hit me in the shoulder, leaving more ink on me. After that I hit him."

"It ain't so!" roared Peter Slade.

"That's the truth," said several. "Peter's hand is full of ink."

"He knocked over an inkwell just before Dick came along," said Fred. "I saw him do it."

"So did I," added Songbird.

"Did you see it?" questioned Captain Putnam of the instructor.

"I saw nothing until the boys were fighting in the aisle," answered the teacher who had been delivering the lecture.

"Captain Putnam, I am sure Dick Rover is not to blame," said a very quiet student named Rames. "Slade put the ink on Rover and struck the first blow—of that I am positive."

"It was my inkwell he knocked over," came from another lad. "I told him to leave it alone, but he wouldn't mind me."

"Oh, you are all against me!" roared Peter Slade.

"Evidently you are guilty," said the master of the Hall, sternly. "I want both you and Richard Rover to come to my office. Rames, you can come, too, and you also, Brocton."

In the office a thorough investigation was held. Several other cadets were called upon to testify, and it was proved that Peter Slade was entirely to blame for what had occurred.

"You should not have attacked him, Richard," said the captain to Dick. "But under the circumstances I cannot blame you. You may go."

For his misconduct Peter Slade was confined in the "guardhouse" for three days. The black eye Dick had given him did not go away very fast and when he came out and resumed his place among the students he was a sight to behold. That he was very angry at the eldest Rover boy is easily imagined.

"I'll fix him some day," he muttered.

"Dick, you want to watch Slade," said Tom, one day, on passing the bully in the hallway.

"I guess you had better watch him yourself, Tom."

"I am going to do that, don't fear. What did the captain do about your mussed-up uniform?"

"Made Slade pay for having it cleaned."

"Did he do it?"

"He had to do it—Captain Putnam put it on the bill to his folks."

"That was right."

"Of course it was. But I understand it made Slade as mad as hops. Oh, he surely has it in for us," went on Dick, and there the subject was dropped.

CHAPTER XXVII

ON THE LAKE

Almost before the boys knew it winter was gone and spring was at hand. The ice on the lake disappeared like magic, and the hills back of Putnam Hall took on a fresh greenness pleasant to behold.

With the coming of warm weather the cadets spent a large part of their off time outdoors. Some took up rowing, and among the number were Sam and Tom. Larry Colby had become the owner of a fair-sized sloop, and he frequently took some of his chums out for a cruise up or down the lake.

"Do you know what I'd like to do?" said Dick one day. "I'd like to visit that old Sobber homestead and see how it looks."

"I've often thought of that," answered Sam. "Wonder how we can manage it?"

The matter was talked over in Larry's presence, and the cadet who owned the sloop said they might make the trip in that craft, provided the master of Putnam Hall would give them the desired permission.

"We'll ask Captain Putnam at once," declared Dick.

Permission was granted to leave Putnam Hall early on the following Saturday morning, provided the weather was clear, and it was arranged that the party should consist of the three Rover boys, Larry, Fred and Songbird. The captain said he preferred that they come back Saturday night, but they could remain away over Sunday if they found it necessary.

"Do you think we'll get any clew to Merrick and Tad Sobber?" asked Dick, with a faint smile.

"Possibly," answered Captain Putnam, smiling back. "You Rovers are great chaps for finding out things."

The sloop was provided with a tiny cuddy, or cabin, and in this the boys placed a small stock of provisions and also a shotgun and some fishing lines. They left the Hall after breakfast and were glad of the promise of a warm day, with the breeze in just the right direction.

"You fellows will have to tell me where to steer the sloop to," said Larry, after the mainsail had been run up. "I don't know where that old house is."

"We have a general idea where it is," answered Dick. "Of course we may have some trouble finding it. But if we get mixed up, we can go ashore and ask the folks living in that vicinity."

The distance to be covered along the lake shore was in the neighborhood of twelve miles, so the boys had quite a sail before them. They took turns at steering, and said they liked the sloop very much.

About four miles had been covered when the breeze began to die away. This was exasperating, but could not be helped, so the boys made the best of it. As the sloop drifted along they got out some fishing tackle, and it was not long before Sam brought up a fair-sized fish, of which he felt quite proud.

"At this rate it will take us till night to reach that old house," remarked Dick, after they had been fishing half an hour. "It is too bad! I thought we'd get there by noon when we started, even if the breeze did go down."

"Oh, I think the breeze will start up again before long," said Tom hopefully. "Let us enjoy this fishing while we have the chance," he added, having just pulled in a real piscatorial prize.

By noon they had a good mess of fish to their credit, and then Sam proposed that they go ashore and build a fire and cook some for dinner.

"There is no use of mourning over the wind," said he.

"If it wasn't for the sloop we might tramp to the old house," returned Dick.

"I shouldn't wish to leave my boat just anywhere," said Larry. "Somebody might run off with her,—and she cost quite some money."

"You might leave her in care of some farmer along here," suggested Songbird, and then he added softly:

"For what is a boat without a breeze?
It's like a forest minus its trees.
It's like a table without a leg,—"

"Or a big blue top without its peg!"

finished Tom. "But I move we camp and cook fish," he

continued. "We can have a dandy meal, along with the stuff we brought along."

The idea of going ashore prevailed, and soon they had tied up the sloop and lowered the mainsail. Brushwood was handy, and having started a fire they cleaned some of the fish and set it to broiling. They had a pot along in which they made coffee, and they also brought out some bread and crackers, cake, and some fruit. They had some meat with them, but left that for possible future use.

The cadets took their time over the meal, and it was not until two o'clock that they again boarded the *Polly*, as Larry had named his craft.

"I think the breeze is coming again," cried Dick, holding up his hand.

"Let it come!" was the cry, and as the wind freshened all felt much better. Soon the *Polly* was bowling over the lake as speedily as when they had first started.

"Do you know what I think?" said Songbird, who stood at the stern looking toward the distant hills. "I think we are going to have more wind than we'll want before night."

"Do you think a big blow is coming?" questioned Fred.

"It looks that way to me. Do you see those dark clouds just beginning to show themselves yonder?"

"Well, I shan't mind a little blow," said Dick. "In fact, I think I'd rather like the excitement." And the others said the same.

They were still about two miles from the spot where they supposed the old house was located, when it suddenly grew darker and the breeze freshened greatly. Then came a puff of air that sent the *Polly* far over on her side.

"Hi! this won't do!" cried Fred, in alarm. "We don't want to upset!"

"Maybe we had better take in some sail," added Songbird nervously.

He had scarcely spoken when there came another puff of wind that made all cling fast to the deck to keep from being pitched overboard. The sky was now very dark, and there were a few flakes of snow in the air.

"It's a spring snowsquall, that's what it is," announced Dick. "I don't think it will last over ten or fifteen minutes."

"It's too much for the *Polly*," came from Larry. "Put down the mainsail, will you?"

Several sprang to do as requested, and hardly had the sheet been lowered and stowed away when there came a fierce gust that drove them well in shore.

"There is a cove—we can go in there for shelter!" cried Sam, and the sloop was steered accordingly. The cove was well protected by trees and they came to anchor at a spot that looked particularly inviting.

The boys were afraid it would rain, and wondered what they would do to keep from getting wet, since the cuddy on the sloop was too small to hold more than two or three of the party. But no rain came, and soon the flurry of snow disappeared. The wind, however, instead of letting up, blew harder than ever.

Arthur M. Winfield

"I am glad we are not out in the middle of the lake," observed Fred. "We'd be capsized sure!"

"This is certainly getting to be a regular gale," answered Dick. "And the worst of it is, there is no telling how long it is going to last."

There was nothing to do but to wait, and in order to keep warm the cadets put up a bit of sailcloth on the deck of the sloop and taking in the cuddy. There they crouched, and told stories and talked for over an hour.

"I move we go on," said Tom, at last. "The wind isn't quite as strong as it was."

Although doubtful of the wisdom of the proceedings, the others voted to proceed and they poled their way out of the cove. Only the jib of the *Polly* was hoisted and this sent them bowling along at a fair rate of speed.

Dick stood in the bow and at last called upon Larry to turn the sloop toward shore.

"I think we must be in the neighborhood of that house now," he said. "And just ahead is a fine cove where the sloop will be as well sheltered as it was at the other cove."

Accordingly Larry turned the *Polly* in, and the other lads lowered the sail. They came to anchor between a number of tall trees, where the sloop was almost screened from sight.

Having made certain the boat could not drift away, the six boys, led by Dick, made their way along the shore until they struck something of a path. Coming to a slight rise, Dick pointed with his hand.

"Isn't that a house, on the other side of the hill?" he asked.

"Yes!" cried Tom. "And by the appearance of it I should say it's the place we are looking for!"

Arthur M. Winfield

CHAPTER XXVIII

AT THE OLD HOUSE

The Rover boys and their chums approached the old house with a good deal of interest. Dick led the way, setting a pace that made it hard for the others to keep up.

"Don't hurry so, Dick," remonstrated Fred. "The house isn't going to run away."

"Dick wants to make sure if that Merrick is around," responded Songbird. "And I can't blame him."

The old Sobber homestead was surrounded by a grove of trees equally aged. One of the trees had blown down, taking a corner of the roof with it. Through this opening the birds flitted.

"I don't believe a soul is around," observed Tom, as they halted in front of the building.

"Nothing like ringing the bell!" cried Sam, and mounting the dilapidated piazza he raised the ancient knocker of the door and used it vigorously. Then came a crash and the youngest Rover felt the piazza bottom give way.

"Look out, a post is coming down!" cried Dick, warningly, and Sam had just time enough to leap away when the corner post of the piazza fell, allowing the roof above to sag several inches.

"Looks to me as if the whole building was on the verge of collapse," was Songbird's comment.

"Yes, and I don't know whether I want to go in or not," added Larry.

"It certainly does look shaky," admitted Dick. "I don't think anybody would risk staying in it long."

Leaving the front, they walked around the old house and gazed through several of the broken-out windows. Inside all was dirt and cobwebs, with a few pieces of broken-down furniture scattered about. As he looked in one window Tom saw a big rat scurry across the floor.

"I guess rats are the only tenants," he said dryly. "And they don't pay rent."

"With a few birds on the top floor, front," added Sam. "Well, do we go in or not?"

"I am going in," declared Dick, and pushed open the old kitchen door. It was damp and mouldy in the apartment, for the rain had soaked loose much of the plaster and caused it to fall.

The big open fireplace looked grimy and forbidding with its iron bars and chains. An iron kettle stood on the chimney-piece, a crack across the bottom.

"Somebody has had a fire here not so very long ago!" said

Dick, and picked up a bit of half-burnt newspaper. He turned it over. "Here is a date. This newspaper is only four days old!"

"Then whoever made a fire here visited this house within the past four days," said Larry in a tragic whisper.

"Whoop! just listen to what a detective Larry is becoming!" cried Tom. "Regular Bowery Bob, the Newsboy Sleuth!"

"Perhaps it was only some curiosity seeker who came here," suggested Fred.

With caution, for the floors were very rotten, the cadets moved from one room of the old house to another.

"Anything in there?" asked Tom of Sam, as the latter peered into a room that was extra dark.

"I can't make out," was the answer, and Sam took a step forward. Then of a sudden there was a strange whirring, and something hit the youngest Rover boy on the ear, causing him to fall back in fright.

"Stop that!" he cried.

"What was it?" queried Tom, while the others came running to the spot.

"Something hit me on the ear!"

"Anybody in there?"

"There must be."

"Come out of that, whoever you are!" yelled Fred, while

Dick pointed his shotgun at the door.

There was no answer, but a second later came the whirring again, and then a big bat flew into the light, just grazing Tom's face.

"A bat!"

"Let it go!" said Songbird, and then the bat flew out of a window and disappeared.

"Oh!" murmured Sam, and breathed a sigh of relief. "I—I thought somebody struck at me!"

"I've got one of those electric pocket lights along," said Tom. "Let me use that."

He turned on the little electric lamp, and by its rays they inspected the apartment. It was a bedroom, and in one corner was an old bedstead and on it a musty straw mattress. In another corner was a closet containing several shelves.

"Here is an old inkwell," said Dick, and brought it forth. "And here are the remains of a box of writing paper and envelopes."

"Any letters?" asked Fred.

They looked around, but at first could find no writings of any kind. But behind one of the shelves, in a crack, they discovered several sheets of paper and took these to the light to read.

"They are parts of letters from Mr. Sobber to his wife," said Dick. "They must have been written by Tad's father."

"He speaks here of Merrick," added Tom, who was scanning a blurred page. "Merrick is Mrs. Sobber's brother beyond a doubt."

"From these letters I should say Mr. Sobber had been off on a sea trip," continued the eldest Rover boy. "And it looks to me as if he had been an honest man, for he tells his wife that he hopes Merrick will give up his gambling habits."

From the bedroom the boys entered what had been the parlor of the house. This was almost bare. To one side of the parlor was an entry-way, and here was a stairs leading to the second story and another leading to the cellar.

"Well, shall we go up or down?" queried Dick.

"Let us see what the cellar looks like first," answered Sam. "Perhaps we'll find a pot of gold there."

"Or a few skeletons," put in Tom.

"Ugh! don't say skeletons," cried Songbird, with a shiver. "I've got the creeps already!"

"Look out that you don't break your neck on the stairs," warned Larry, and then Dick led the way down, holding the light before him.

If it was damp above it was far more so below, and the boys shivered in spite of themselves. The cellar had only a mud bottom and this was covered with slime and mold. There was little there to interest them outside of an old chest which, when they pried it open, proved to be empty.

"Listen!" cried Tom, suddenly, and held up his hand.

"What did you hear?" demanded several of the others.

"I thought I heard somebody walking around upstairs. There it is again!"

All gave attention, and heard the unmistakable sounds of footsteps on the stairs leading to the second story.

"Who is up there?" called out Dick, and turned to leave the cellar, followed by his brothers and chums.

"Stay where you are!" came back in a harsh voice. "Don't any of you dare to come out of that cellar!"

"It is Merrick!" burst out Tom.

Hardly had he spoken when they heard a door shut sharply and a bolt dropped into place. Then the footsteps retreated.

"He has shut the door to the cellar!" cried Dick, flashing the light upward. "We are locked in!"

"Hark! I heard more than one person running from the house," said Larry.

"That Pike must be with him."

"Or else Tad Sobber."

As quickly as he could, Dick ran up the old stairs and tried the door. It was in fairly good condition and refused to budge.

"Smash it down!" called out Tom, and went to his brother's assistance.

"We must get out and collar those rascals," said Sam. "Can't you get the door open?"

"We ought to be able to," answered Dick. "Here, catch the light and take the gun."

In a few seconds Dick, Tom and Songbird were pressing on the door with all their strength. All stood on the top step of the cellar stairs.

"Now then, all together!" cried Dick, and they shoved with might and main. Then came a crack below them, and an instant later the cellar stairs collapsed, carrying them with it. As they went down in a confused heap the stairs struck the electric light and smashed it. It also knocked the shotgun from Sam's hand.

Bang! went the firearm, with a report in the narrow confines of the cellar that was deafening.

"I'm killed! I'm killed!" came from Larry, an instant later. "You've shot my hand off!"

CHAPTER XXIX

A WRECK AND A CAPTURE

"Get off of my fingers!"

"Please let me get out of this hole!"

"Say, how can I get up if you're going to sit on my legs?"

These and a few more utterances came from the boys as they endeavored to clear themselves of the wreckage of the fallen stairs. The small cellar was filled with smoke from the shot-gun, and Larry was dancing around flipping his hurt hand in the air. All was pitch dark, for the small windows were covered with dirt and cobwebs to such a depth that no light penetrated through them.

"Beware of that gun!" called Dick, when he could speak. "Only one barrel went off, remember."

"Larry, are you really killed?" questioned Sara, who, somehow, felt responsible, since the weapon had been in his hands.

"N—no, but I'm hit in the fingers," came from the wounded boy. "The shot went right past my head, too!"

Arthur M. Winfield

"Make a light, somebody," called out Fred. "Songbird, you've got some matches."

The poet of the Hall lit a match, and by this faint light the boys first of all looked at Larry's damaged hand. Fortunately the charge of shot had merely grazed the thumb and middle finger, and it was found that Larry was more frightened than hurt. The hand was bound up in a couple of handkerchiefs.

"When we get back to the boat you'll want to wash the wounds well," said Dick.

Tom had picked up the electric pocket light, but found he could not make it work. Again they were in darkness until another match was lit.

"We can't reach that door, with the stairs down," was Dick's comment. "Let us break out a window."

This was easily accomplished, and one after another the cadets crawled forth from the cellar. It was a tight squeeze, especially for Fred, who was rather large at the waist line.

"I guess those fellows who ran away thought we couldn't get through that window," said Songbird.

"If it had been an inch smaller I should have been stuck," answered Fred.

They looked all around the old building, but nobody was in sight. The front door stood wide open, and they rightly surmised that the others had taken their departure that way.

"The question is, Which way did they go?" came from Dick.

"Do you think they went on foot?" asked Sam. "They might

have a carriage."

"Or a boat," added Larry. "Oh, I hope we can catch them, just to make 'em pay for these hurt fingers of mine!" And he shut his teeth hard, for the wounds pained him not a little.

"Larry, I trust you don't think it was my fault," observed Sam.

"Not a bit of it, Sam. It was simply an accident, that's all. I am glad those on the stairs didn't hurt themselves."

"Well, my knee doesn't feel any too good," came from Tom. "I guess I scratched it quite some."

"Shall we try to find those fellows first or go upstairs and look around?" asked Songbird.

"Let us try to find them first," said Dick. "We can come back here any time."

"I have a plan," said Tom. "Let us scatter in all directions. If anybody sees anything of them, give the school whistle."

"Good! that's the talk!" exclaimed Sam. "The sooner the better."

In a minute more the six cadets were hunting in as many different directions for those they were after. Larry, Songbird and Fred took to the lake shore, while the three Rover boys went up and down the roadway and into the woods beyond.

Nearly half an hour was spent in the search when the other lads heard a whistle from the lake shore. The signal came from Larry, and was repeated several times.

Arthur M. Winfield

"He wants us in a hurry," said Sam to Dick, when they met, and started on a run. They met Larry coming towards them, beckoning wildly.

"Hurry up!" he called.

"What's up?" asked Dick.

"They just went past in a sailboat and they are bound across the lake."

"The two men?" asked Sam.

"Yes, and Tad Sobber, too."

"Tad!"

"Yes. Their boat couldn't have been very far from mine. I saw the two men get on board and then Tad came from a cabin, and all three hoisted the sails as quickly as they could and stood over in the direction of the point with the three rocks—you remember the spot?"

"I do—the place we once went nutting," said Dick.

By this time the other cadets were coming up, and they listened with keen interest to what Larry had to tell. In the meantime all ran to the *Polly*, and the sloop was poled out of the cove and the mainsail and jib were hoisted. As Larry was in no condition to steer, Dick took the tiller.

"They will get away if they possibly can," observed Songbird. "Do you think, if we get too close to them, they'll fire at us, or anything like that?"

"There is no telling," answered Dick. "But I am going to load up that empty barrel of the shotgun, and if they dare to shoot I'll shoot back," he added, with determination.

The other boat was in sight, but a good half mile away, and it was a serious question whether the *Polly* could get anywhere near the craft before the point with the three rocks was gained.

"Well, if they go ashore we can capture the boat anyway," observed Sam. "That will be something."

"Probably the boat was only hired. The owner may not know what rascals those chaps are."

"The craft looked old and clumsy to me," said Larry. "If you sail the *Polly* with care perhaps you can catch her—if they don't play us some trick."

The chase was now on in earnest, and the cadets on board the sloop did all in their power to make speed. There was a fair breeze, the gale having gone down while they were at the house.

"I don't think they know much about running a boat," said Tom, presently. "What are they up to now?"

"They are turning back!" cried Sam. "See, they are headed for yonder cove. They are not going up to the three rocks."

"What cove is that?" asked Songbird. "Is it the place we went fishing the day we caught the turtle?"

"Yes."

"Then they had better look out! Don't you remember those sharp rocks, right near the mouth of the cove?"

Arthur M. Winfield

Those who had been fishing the day mentioned did remember the rocks, and they watched the boat ahead with keen interest. The wind had freshened a little and the craft had swung around swiftly and was rushing for the cove. They could see one of the men trying to lower the mainsail.

"They are in dangerous water!" cried Dick.

He had just uttered the words when they saw the boat strike something, shiver from stem to stern, and back away. Then she went ahead and struck a second time. A second later she went over to larboard, throwing the two men and Tad Sobber into the lake!

"They've struck the rocks!"

"The boat is sinking!"

"They are all in the water!"

"Lower the mainsail!" yelled Larry. "We don't want to get caught on the rocks! Sheer off, Dick!"

Dick swung the tiller around, and in a few seconds the mainsail came down with a bang and was secured by the others. The jib was still up, and this drew just sufficiently to send them forward slowly, to the spot where the catastrophe had occurred.

They found Pike floundering around in the water, yelling lustily for aid. Sid Merrick and Tad Sobber had struck out for the nearest part of the shore, about two hundred feet away.

"Here, catch hold of this and I'll pull you up," said Tom, reaching down to Pike with a pole. The floundering man did as told willingly, and was quickly hauled to the deck. Then the *Polly* was turned toward the shore and the jib was lowered.

It was no easy task to bring the sloop in, for they had to beware of the rocks, and by the time this was accomplished Sid Merrick and Tad Sobber had landed and were running for the woods with all possible speed. Dick raised his shotgun and fired to scare them, but they kept on, and in a few minutes disappeared from sight.

Arthur M. Winfield

CHAPTER XXX

GOOD-BYE TO PUTNAM HALL

Leaving John Pike in charge of the others, the three Rover boys set off after Sobber and Merrick. They followed the trail for awhile with ease, for the fugitives were dripping wet from their involuntary bath.

"We have one advantage," said Dick, as they ran along. "Being wet they will attract attention, and we'll be able to follow them up that way."

About a quarter of a mile was covered when they heard a crashing in the brushwood not far ahead of them. Then came a yell of pain from both Merrick and Tad Sobber.

"Ouch! I'm being stung to death!"

"Get off of me! Oh! oh! oh!"

"They are hornets, Tad! Run, or they'll be after us!"

"I—I can't run! Oh! one stung me in the eye!" screamed Tad Sobber.

Then the Rover boys heard the man and the boy plunge on,

Tad screaming with pain at every step.

"Wait! we can't go that way!" cried Tom, who had no desire to tumble into the hornets' nest as the others had probably done. "Let's go around!" And he leaped to the left.

As they progressed they heard Tad Sobber still crying wildly, and they heard Sid Merrick urging him to run faster.

"I'm stung, too—in about a dozen places!" said the bond thief. "But we mustn't be captured."

"Oh, it is awful!" groaned Tad. "I can hardly bear the pain!" And he went on, clutching his uncle by the arm. Both were indeed in a sorry plight.

But coming out on a road, fortune favored them. They met a colored man running a touring car. He was alone and they quickly hired him to take them to the nearest town.

"We fell into the lake by accident," said Sid Merrick. "We want to get where we can change our clothing."

"And get something for these hornet stings," added Tad Sobber. "If I don't get something soon I'll go crazy from pain."

As the three Rover boys ran towards the roadway Dick saw a big, flat pocketbook lying on the ground. He darted for it and picked it up.

"Merrick must have dropped this," he said. "It's wet, and here is a dead hornet stuck fast to it. Guess the hornets made him forget that he had it."

Slipping the pocketbook into his pocket, Dick ran out on the

Arthur M. Winfield

roadway and looked up and down. But Merrick and Sobber were gone, and what had become of them the boys did not learn until the next day, and then it was too late.

"What's in that pocketbook?" asked Sam, after the hunt had come to an end for the time being.

"We'll soon learn," said his big brother, and opened up the still wet leather. Inside were several bank bills and a fat envelope.

"Uncle Randolph's missing traction company bonds!" cried Dick, bringing them forth. "This is the best ever!"

"Are they all there?" asked Tom.

Dick counted them over rapidly.

"Yes—ten for one thousand dollars each."

"Hurrah!" shouted Sam. "Won't Uncle Randolph be glad when he hears of this!"

The boys were highly elated over the find, and now they had the bonds they concluded that a further search for Sid Merrick could wait. They did not care whether Tad Sobber was captured or not, as they did not think the bully was much of a criminal.

When they got back to the sloop they found that the others had bound John Pike's hands behind him. The robber was very meek, and he declared that Sid Merrick was to blame for everything.

"He wanted to sell the bonds many times," said Pike. "But he knew that Mr. Rover had advertised the numbers in the newspapers and he was afraid to do it. He said he would wait until the affair blew over. Then he was going to sell out, divide up, and go to Europe."

Pike added that the boat had belonged to himself. She was an old craft and was allowed to remain on the rocks. It came out later that Pike had formerly lived on the lake shore and had thus become acquainted with Merrick and the Sobbers.

As soon as possible the captured robber was handed over to the authorities, and Dick sent a message home acquainting his uncle with what had occurred. This brought on both Randolph Rover and the boys' father.

"You have certainly done wonderfully well," said Randolph Rover, as he took his bonds. "Were you not so rich already I should want to reward you."

"We don't want any reward," said Dick. "But I am sorry we didn't catch Merrick."

For a long time the authorities tried to catch Sid Merrick and also endeavored to learn the whereabouts of Tad Sobber, but without success. They had disappeared, and that seemed to be the end of it. The old house was visited again, but nothing of value was found there. Later on some tramps set it on fire and it was burnt to the ground. A month later John Pike and one other freight thief who was captured were tried for their misdeeds and sent to prison. The authorities used Bill Dangler as a witness against them, and Dangler, cones- quently, was let go. Strange to say, Dangler turned over a new leaf and became a hard working man in a railroad stone quarry some miles from Carwell.

With the mystery of the traction company bonds cleared up, the Rover boys returned to Putnam Hall to complete their

last term at that institution of learning. They applied themselves diligently to their studies, and when the final examina-
tions came off all passed with flying colors.

"Whoop! I'm glad those exams are over!" cried Tom. "I feel
as if a hundred-pound weight was taken off my shoulders."

"I am glad, too," answered Sam.

"And I am glad all of us did so well," put in Dick. "Our
reports will please father and Uncle Randolph and Aunt
Martha."

It had been arranged that the commencement exercises
should be carried out on rather an elaborate scale, and many
people were invited to attend. This brought all the Rovers
and also the Stanhopes and the Lanings to Putnam Hall. Dick
had been called on to deliver the valedictory and he made
such a stirring address that he was vigorously applauded.
Sam and Tom appeared in a humor dialogue, with Fred and
Larry, and this was received with shouts of laughter.
Songbird recited an original poem which was a vast
improvement over the most of his doggerel, and Hans and
some of the others sang in a quartet which would have done
credit to the average college glee club.

"Oh, it was splendid, Dick!" said Dora, after it was over and
congratulations were in order. And her eyes shone like stars
as she pressed his hand.

"I saw only you, Dora, when I got up to speak," he
whispered. "And that's why I did my best."

"You and Sam had better go on the stage," said Nellie to
Tom. "That dialogue was too funny for anything!"

"I laughed till the tears came," added Grace. "It was a splendid programme all the way through."

"Well done, my boys, well done," said Anderson Rover, as he took each by the hand. "I was never so proud of you as I am to-day."

"Now that we have finished our studies here what are we to do next?" questioned Dick, earnestly.

"We will settle that question this summer," answered his father. "But in the meantime—" Mr. Rover paused and looked at his oldest son thoughtfully.

"But what, father?"

"I will tell you when we get home, Dick—there is no use of my trying to do so in this excitement. I have something very unusual to propose," answered Anderson Rover, and what that proposal was, and what came of it, will be related in another volume, to be entitled, "The Rover Boys on Treasure Isle; Or, The Strange Cruise of the Steam Yacht." In that volume we shall meet many of our old friends again, and also learn something concerning the disappearance of Sid Merrick and Tad Sobber.

That evening the celebration at Putnam Hall was continued. The cadets lit a huge bonfire on the campus and around this they danced and sang and made speeches. They cheered everybody, from Captain Putnam down to Peleg Snuggers, and the festivities were kept up until midnight. Then the boys went to bed—but not to sleep—for was this not the last night at school? Innumerable tricks were played, including one on Peter Slade that that youth never forgot. This made the bully so angry he declared he was going to quit Putnam Hall for good, and he did, and nobody missed him.

Arthur M. Winfield

"And now for home!" cried Dick the next morning on dressing.

"And fresh adventures," added Tom.

"But I do hate to leave dear old Putnam Hall," sighed Sam, and then the others sighed, too.

It was not until noon that the three Rover boys were ready to go, having first bid farewell to their numerous friends. Then they shook hands with Captain Putnam.

"We hate awfully to leave you," said Dick, earnestly.

"And I hate to have you go, Richard," was the reply. "You must visit the Hall some time in the future."

"And you must come and see us, Captain Putnam," said Tom.

"Yes, indeed," added Sam.

"I will," answered the master of the Hall.

Then the boys shook hands all over again and ran for the carryall. Some boys left behind set up a shout:

"Good-bye, Dick!"

"Sorry to have you go, Tom!"

"May we meet again, Sam!"

"Good-bye, everybody!" was the answering shout. "Good-bye to dear old Putnam Hall!"

Then the whip cracked, the carryall rolled from the door; and the Rover boys' days at Putnam Hall military school were at an end.

THE END

Arthur M. Winfield

Other books by this author

The Mystery at Putnam Hall

The Rover Boys at Colby Hall

The Rover Boys at College

The Rover Boys at School

The Rover Boys in New York

The Rover Boys in the Air

The Rover Boys in the Jungle

The Rover Boys In The Mountains

The Rover Boys on Land and Sea

The Rover Boys on the Great Lakes

The Rover Boys on the Ocean

The Rover Boys on the River

The Rover Boys out West

The Rover Boys on a Hunt

Choose from Thousands of 1stWorldLibrary Classics By

A. M. Barnard
Ada Leverson
Adolphus William Ward
Aesop
Agatha Christie
Alexander Aaronsohn
Alexander Kielland
Alexandre Dumas
Alfred Gatty
Alfred Ollivant
Alice Duer Miller
Alice Turner Curtis
Alice Dunbar
Allen Chapman
Alleyne Ireland
Ambrose Bierce
Amelia E. Barr
Amory H. Bradford
Andrew Lang
Andrew McFarland Davis
Andy Adams
Angela Brazil
Anna Alice Chapin
Anna Sewell
Annie Besant
Annie Hamilton Donnell
Annie Payson Call
Annie Roe Carr
Annonaymous
Anton Chekhov
Archibald Lee Fletcher
Arnold Bennett
Arthur C. Benson
Arthur Conan Doyle
Arthur M. Winfield
Arthur Ransome
Arthur Schnitzler
Arthur Train
Atticus
B.H. Baden-Powell
B. M. Bower
B. C. Chatterjee
Baroness Emmuska Orczy
Baroness Orczy
Basil King
Bayard Taylor
Ben Macomber
Bertha Muzzy Bower
Bjornstjerne Bjornson

Booth Tarkington
Boyd Cable
Bram Stoker
C. Collodi
C. E. Orr
C. M. Ingleby
Carolyn Wells
Catherine Parr Traill
Charles A. Eastman
Charles Amory Beach
Charles Dickens
Charles Dudley Warner
Charles Farrar Browne
Charles Ives
Charles Kingsley
Charles Klein
Charles Hanson Towne
Charles Lathrop Pack
Charles Romyn Dake
Charles Whibley
Charles Willing Beale
Charlotte M. Braeme
Charlotte M. Yonge
Charlotte Perkins Stetson
Clair W. Hayes
Clarence Day Jr.
Clarence E. Mulford
Clemence Housman
Confucius
Coningsby Dawson
Cornelis DeWitt Wilcox
Cyril Burleigh
D. H. Lawrence
Daniel Defoe
David Garnett
Dinah Craik
Don Carlos Janes
Donald Keyhoe
Dorothy Kilner
Dougan Clark
Douglas Fairbanks
E. Nesbit
E. P. Roe
E. Phillips Oppenheim
E. S. Brooks
Earl Barnes
Edgar Rice Burroughs
Edith Van Dyne
Edith Wharton

Edward Everett Hale
Edward J. O'Biren
Edward S. Ellis
Edwin L. Arnold
Eleanor Atkins
Eleanor Hallowell Abbott
Eliot Gregory
Elizabeth Gaskell
Elizabeth McCracken
Elizabeth Von Arnim
Ellem Key
Emerson Hough
Emilie F. Carlen
Emily Bronte
Emily Dickinson
Enid Bagnold
Enilor Macartney Lane
Erasmus W. Jones
Ernie Howard Pie
Ethel May Dell
Ethel Turner
Ethel Watts Mumford
Eugene Sue
Eugenie Foa
Eugene Wood
Eustace Hale Ball
Evelyn Everett-green
Everard Cotes
F. H. Cheley
F. J. Cross
F. Marion Crawford
Fannie E. Newberry
Federick Austin Ogg
Ferdinand Ossendowski
Fergus Hume
Florence A. Kilpatrick
Fremont B. Deering
Francis Bacon
Francis Darwin
Frances Hodgson Burnett
Frances Parkinson Keyes
Frank Gee Patchin
Frank Harris
Frank Jewett Mather
Frank L. Packard
Frank V. Webster
Frederic Stewart Isham
Frederick Trevor Hill
Frederick Winslow Taylor

Friedrich Kerst	Hayden Carruth	James Branch Cabell
Friedrich Nietzsche	Helent Hunt Jackson	James DeMille
Fyodor Dostoyevsky	Helen Nicolay	James Joyce
G.A. Henty	Hendrik Conscience	James Lane Allen
G.K. Chesterton	Hendy David Thoreau	James Lane Allen
Gabrielle E. Jackson	Henri Barbusse	James Oliver Curwood
Garrett P. Serviss	Henrik Ibsen	James Oppenheim
Gaston Leroux	Henry Adams	James Otis
George A. Warren	Henry Ford	James R. Driscoll
George Ade	Henry Frost	Jane Abbott
Geroge Bernard Shaw	Henry James	Jane Austen
George Cary Eggleston	Henry Jones Ford	Jane L. Stewart
George Durston	Henry Seton Merriman	Janet Aldridge
George Ebers	Henry W Longfellow	Jens Peter Jacobsen
George Eliot	Herbert A. Giles	Jerome K. Jerome
George Gissing	Herbert Carter	Jessie Graham Flower
George MacDonald	Herbert N. Casson	John Buchan
George Meredith	Herman Hesse	John Burroughs
George Orwell	Hildegard G. Frey	John Cournos
George Sylvester Viereck	Homer	John F. Kennedy
George Tucker	Honore De Balzac	John Gay
George W. Cable	Horace B. Day	John Glasworthy
George Wharton James	Horace Walpole	John Habberton
Gertrude Atherton	Horatio Alger Jr.	John Joy Bell
Gordon Casserly	Howard Pyle	John Kendrick Bangs
Grace E. King	Howard R. Garis	John Milton
Grace Gallatin	Hugh Lofting	John Philip Sousa
Grace Greenwood	Hugh Walpole	John Taintor Foote
Grant Allen	Humphry Ward	Jonas Lauritz Idemil Lie
Guillermo A. Sherwell	Ian Maclaren	Jonathan Swift
Gulielma Zollinger	Inez Haynes Gillmore	Joseph A. Altsheler
Gustav Flaubert	Irving Bacheller	Joseph Carey
H. A. Cody	Isabel Cecilia Williams	Joseph Conrad
H. B. Irving	Isabel Hornibrook	Joseph E. Badger Jr
H. C. Bailey	Israel Abrahams	Joseph Hergesheimer
H. G. Wells	Ivan Turgenev	Joseph Jacobs
H. H. Munro	J. G.Austin	Jules Vernes
H. Irving Hancock	J. Henri Fabre	Julian Hawthrone
H. R. Naylor	J. M. Barrie	Julie A Lippmann
H. Rider Haggard	J. M. Walsh	Justin Huntly McCarthy
H. W. C. Davis	J. Macdonald Oxley	Kakuzo Okakura
Haldeman Julius	J. R. Miller	Karle Wilson Baker
Hall Caine	J. S. Fletcher	Kate Chopin
Hamilton Wright Mabie	J. S. Knowles	Kenneth Grahame
Hans Christian Andersen	J. Storer Clouston	Kenneth McGaffey
Harold Avery	J. W. Duffield	Kate Langley Bosher
Harold McGrath	Jack London	Kate Langley Bosher
Harriet Beecher Stowe	Jacob Abbott	Katherine Cecil Thurston
Harry Castlemon	James Allen	Katherine Stokes
Harry Coghill	James Andrews	L. A. Abbot
Harry Houidini	James Baldwin	L. T. Meade

L. Frank Baum
Latta Griswold
Laura Dent Crane
Laura Lee Hope
Laurence Housman
Lawrence Beasley
Leo Tolstoy
Leonid Andreyev
Lewis Carroll
Lewis Sperry Chafer
Lilian Bell
Lloyd Osbourne
Louis Hughes
Louis Joseph Vance
Louis Tracy
Louisa May Alcott
Lucy Fitch Perkins
Lucy Maud Montgomery
Luther Benson
Lydia Miller Middleton
Lyndon Orr
M. Corvus
M. H. Adams
Margaret E. Sangster
Margret Howth
Margaret Vandercook
Margaret W. Hungerford
Margret Penrose
Maria Edgeworth
Maria Thompson Daviess
Mariano Azuela
Marion Polk Angellotti
Mark Overton
Mark Twain
Mary Austin
Mary Catherine Crowley
Mary Cole
Mary Hastings Bradley
Mary Roberts Rinehart
Mary Rowlandson
M. Wollstonecraft Shelley
Maud Lindsay
Max Beerbohm
Myra Kelly
Nathaniel Hawthrone
Nicolo Machiavelli
O. F. Walton
Oscar Wilde
Owen Johnson
P.G. Wodehouse
Paul and Mabel Thorne

Paul G. Tomlinson
Paul Severing
Percy Brebner
Percy Keese Fitzhugh
Peter B. Kyne
Plato
Quincy Allen
R. Derby Holmes
R. L. Stevenson
R. S. Ball
Rabindranath Tagore
Rahul Alvares
Ralph Bonehill
Ralph Henry Barbour
Ralph Victor
Ralph Waldo Emmerson
Rene Descartes
Ray Cummings
Rex Beach
Rex E. Beach
Richard Harding Davis
Richard Jefferies
Richard Le Gallienne
Robert Barr
Robert Frost
Robert Gordon Anderson
Robert L. Drake
Robert Lansing
Robert Lynd
Robert Michael Ballantyne
Robert W. Chambers
Rosa Nouchette Carey
Rudyard Kipling
Saint Augustine
Samuel B. Allison
Samuel Hopkins Adams
Sarah Bernhardt
Sarah C. Hallowell
Selma Lagerlof
Sherwood Anderson
Sigmund Freud
Standish O'Grady
Stanley Weyman
Stella Benson
Stella M. Francis
Stephen Crane
Stewart Edward White
Stijn Streuvels
Swami Abhedananda
Swami Parmananda
T. S. Ackland

T. S. Arthur
The Princess Der Ling
Thomas A. Janvier
Thomas A Kempis
Thomas Anderton
Thomas Bailey Aldrich
Thomas Bulfinch
Thomas De Quincey
Thomas Dixon
Thomas H. Huxley
Thomas Hardy
Thomas More
Thornton W. Burgess
U. S. Grant
Upton Sinclair
Valentine Williams
Various Authors
Vaughan Kester
Victor Appleton
Victor G. Durham
Victoria Cross
Virginia Woolf
Wadsworth Camp
Walter Camp
Walter Scott
Washington Irving
Wilbur Lawton
Wilkie Collins
Willa Cather
Willard F. Baker
William Dean Howells
William le Queux
W. Makepeace Thackeray
William W. Walter
William Shakespeare
Winston Churchill
Yei Theodora Ozaki
Yogi Ramacharaka
Young E. Allison
Zane Grey

www.ingramcontent.com/pod-product-compliance
Lightning Source LLC
Chambersburg PA
CBHW050035180626
46810CB00002B/733